THE BUSBY
BABES

RICHARD SKINNER

URBANE
Publications

First published in Great Britain in 2016
by Urbane Publications Ltd
Suite 3, Brown Europe House,
33/34 Gleamingwood Drive,
Chatham, Kent ME5 8RZ

A CIP catalogue record for this book is available
from the British Library.

Paperback ISBN 978-1-910692-57-8
mobi ISBN 978-1-910692-59-2
epub ISBN 978-1-910692-58-5

Cover design and typeset at Chandler Book Design,
King's Lynn, Norfolk

Front cover image: Getty Images

Printed in Great Britain by
CP Group (UK) Ltd,
Croydon, CR0 4YY

'To the 23 who died.'

"More than merely an account of a tragedy, it is a portrait of an era and a tribute to a group of young men - working class heroes all - whose talent, endeavour and camaraderie transcends football. This is the team that made the English game beautiful, and to rediscover this golden generation is to revisit the foundation, the death, and the rebirth of something magical. Essential reading for fans and non-fans alike."

Stephen Kelman, author of *Pigeon English*

CONTENTS

ACKNOWLEDGEMENTS

Thanks to Jacqueline Crooks, Keith Hutson and Stephen Kelman, and to Niamh Dillon, James Strong and Richard Taylor of Strong Pictures.

Thanks also to Matthew Smith at Urbane.

Lastly, my deepest thanks to Harry Gregg and Albert Scanlon for sharing their memories with me.

3

FOREWORD

This book is a tale of spirit, courage and the eternal bonds of friendship. It is about a group of men whose passion for football led them to unparalleled success and unprecedented glory. But it also cost many of them their lives. Matt Busby, the patriarchal Manager of Manchester United, revolutionised English football by bending the rules and pushing his players to the limits. At Manchester United, he created a team of 'boy wonders', the 'Busby Babes', a group of players who became the game's first superstars, heroes to millions of people. But, just as they were on the verge of world acclaim, disaster struck.

Few today would recognise the names of Tommy Taylor, Roger Byrne or Eddie Colman but, in their day, they were as famous and glamorous as film stars. More than half a century has passed since their premature death and it is time to tell the story of their astonishing achievements to a new generation of adoring football fans. Researched extensively and exhaustively, the book reconstructs in detail the drama of their journey from schoolboys to junior team players, from becoming League

Champions to their glorious efforts in Europe. Supported by Harry Gregg and Albert Scanlon's moving testimony, which breathes life into the memory of those so long dead, the book gives a fuller, more complete picture of the Busby Babes than ever before. This is their definitive story.

Richard Skinner,
February 2016

INTRODUCTION

L ike anyone even remotely interested in football in Britain, I was well aware of Manchester United whilst growing up in the 70s and 80s. They were a glamorous side, the side that everyone wanted to beat. In true British style, they seemed to be the team that everyone hated just because they were so successful. Liverpool and Arsenal were also very successful during these decades, but they simply didn't attract the kind of hostility that United did. During the early to mid-90s, while Liverpool and Arsenal dropped away, Manchester United were the only British team that performed well in the Champions' League, a new club competition that had been set up in 1992 to replace the old European Cup. They regularly got to the quarter-finals, then the semis. In 1999, they at last got to the final. They had already won the Premiership and the FA Cup that year – could they go on to do an incredible Treble? No one who watched that game at the Camp Nou that night will ever forget it. Coming from behind, United scored twice in stoppage time to beat Bayern Munich 2-1. It was a sensational victory and the Treble was amongst the greatest achievements, if not *the* greatest, in the club's long history. The country loved them then.

The core of the team that won the Treble that year had grown up together at United, arriving as kids and playing in the club's youth and reserve teams before breaking through into the first team. Those players are household names now: David Beckham, Nicky Butt, Ryan Giggs, Gary and Philip Neville and Paul Scholes. But there was another Manchester United team, from the 1950s, that people who have a knowledge of the game say was just as good, if not better than the team that won the Treble. That particular group of players was affectionately known as the 'Busby Babes', a name that alluded to their Manager, Matt Busby, and to their extreme youth.

One of the Babes, for instance, was right-winger Johnny Berry. Like Beckham, Berry was a fantastic crosser of the ball, but he could also dribble and take players on, a skill that Beckham lacked. Very similar in temperament to Roy Keane, the ferocious Roger Byrne was every bit as inspirational as Captain. On the left-wing, David Pegg had all the pace and flair of Ryan Giggs. Liam Whelan was another 'fox in the box' in the mould of Paul Scholes, while Tommy Taylor seemed to have a magnet in his head and scored as many headers as Teddy Sheringham.

This Manchester United team, created by Busby during the 1950s, was a team of boy wonders, a group of players who became the game's first superstars, heroes to millions of people. Like the team of 1999, almost all of them had lived and grown up together, playing their way through the club's youth and reserve teams. They all broke into the first team with astonishing speed and achieved immediate success. At the end of the 1955/56 season, Manchester United were crowned League Champions with an average age of just 20 years. It seemed abundantly clear to the whole country that there was nothing this group of young, handsome, gifted players wouldn't achieve over the next decade.

As 1956 League Champions, Manchester United were invited to participate in a fledgling football tournament called the European Cup – they accepted. As the first English side ever to enter the competition, they had an impressive run, beating the likes of Anderlecht, Borussia Dortmund and Atlético Madrid before narrowly losing to Real Madrid, the eventual winners, in the semi-final. Not bad for a bunch of boys from Manchester. The following year, United won the league again and entered the European Cup once more. They reached the quarter-finals, where they were drawn against Red Star Belgrade. United won the first leg at Old Trafford comfortably and, on 4th February 1958, they flew out to Belgrade in a private charter plane to play the return leg. Travelling to Yugoslavia in those days was like visiting a different world, but Manchester United was a famous club in Yugoslavia and the players were treated like royalty everywhere they went. After a thrilling return match, United went through 5-4 on aggregate. They were now just one step away from getting to the European Cup Final but, just as they were on the verge of world acclaim, disaster struck.

The following morning, 6th February 1958, the team and its entourage of staff, pressmen and guests, boarded their British European Airways flight bound for Manchester via Munich, where they would briefly stop to refuel. When they landed in Munich, the weather conditions were atrocious – it was snowing heavily and the runway was covered in slush and ice. Having refuelled, the plane attempted take-off, sliding down the runway as it did so. Just at the critical moment, however, the plane's engines lost power and take-off was abandoned. This happened a second time, at which point the captain decided to return to the terminal and check the aeroplane over. Everything was working normally and so the passengers re-boarded the plane.

On the third take-off, the plane speeded much further down the runway than on the previous two attempts. As the plane edged towards take-off, the engines suddenly lost power again at the critical moment. The pilots looked out the cockpit windows only to see the perimeter fence fast approaching. Attempting to avoid disaster, they braked and lifted the undercarriage, but it was too late – the plane went crashing through the fence, colliding with a house, which ripped the left wing off and split the cabin in two. The rear of the plane went into spin and crashed into a shed containing a fuel truck, a collision that sent a fireball into the sky. In a matter of seconds, the aircraft was a mangled, burning wreck and bodies were strewn across the fields of snow.

Of the 44 passengers on board that day, 21 died instantly, including seven United players. The survivors were taken to hospital in fleets of ambulances. In the weeks after the crash, many of the seriously injured fought desperately for their lives. Miracles were performed by the hospital staff but, despite their magnificent efforts, another two people were to die, including Duncan Edwards, the most gifted footballer of his generation and one of the greatest players ever to have graced the game. Manchester was sent into shock and the world mourned. Never before had the world experienced such a dreadful sporting disaster and, arguably, it still hasn't.

Mention the phrase 'Busby Babes' to people these days, however, and most will look quite puzzled. They think they have heard the name, but won't be sure. Some think it has to do with the Busby Berkeley dancers in 1930s' Hollywood. Most won't even know it is something to do with sport. Once you mention the Munich Air Disaster, however, almost all will begin to nod as the details start to emerge in their minds. 'Ah yes,' they say, 'the Busby Babes', as if they knew all along. The phrase jangles about in our collective memory, like coins in the pocket, an event buried so deeply that it almost needs to be excavated.

The Busby Babes played football in the era just before television, so there is no footage of their performances to speak of. All we have are a few clips and snaps, which is why the testimony and eye-witness accounts of those who survived the crash are so essential. For this book, three of the survivors of the crash, Harry Gregg, Albert Scanlon and Ken Morgans, were interviewed extensively and their statements play a huge part in the telling of this story. It is a story of spirit, courage and the eternal bonds of friendship. It is about a group of men whose passion for football led them to unparalleled success and unprecedented glory, but which ultimately cost many of them their lives. It is a story of human beings conducting themselves at the very highest levels.

But the story really starts long before Munich, with Matt Busby, and his arrival at Manchester United just after the end of the Second World War. The wily, canny Scot spent years laying down the foundations of a team he was convinced would achieve greater glory than any other. His paternal attitude and hands-on approach towards his young charges guaranteed that he had unparalleled levels of control over them. He was compassionate towards them but he could be ruthless when he needed to be. He bent the rules and pushed his players to their limits. Without his dreams, and the grit and toil necessary to make them a reality, none of the following extraordinary events would ever have happened in the first place.

1

MATT BUSBY &
JIMMY MURPHY

I n October 1945, a 36-year-old Scot named Matt Busby arrived at Old Trafford as the new manager of Manchester United Football Club. Newly demobbed from the Army, it was Busby's first job in peacetime Britain. He had signed a five-year contract to take this ailing club back to the upper echelons of English football. The war had wreaked havoc on football clubs and Manchester United was in very poor shape indeed. For a start, they didn't have a pitch to play on. On 11th March 1941, bombs from a German air raid targeting the huge Trafford Park industrial complex went astray and had demolished Old Trafford. The stands had been flattened and were now just piles of rubble. The pitch was pitted with bomb craters and was just a sea of weeds. After the bombing, United put in a claim with the War Damage Commission and were awarded £22,278. It would take another eight years before the ground was rebuilt, however, and until then, United would have to suffer the indignity of renting Maine Road, home to their big rivals Manchester City, and playing their home games there.

Added to that was the fact that, because Old Trafford was in such a state of disrepair, Manchester United FC didn't actually have a base at the ground to operate from. Instead, the club was run out of a small office in a cold storage depot belonging to the chairman, James Gibson. Finances were so tight that Busby had share his room with the club secretary, Walter Crickmer, the man who had been caretaker-manager of the club since 1937, and a young typist borrowed from the chairman's cold storage company. It was hardly an auspicious start, but the conditions were exactly what Busby wanted. He had, in fact, already been offered a job managing Liverpool, with whom he had spent three happy seasons as a player. In those days, Liverpool was a much bigger club than Manchester United in every sense – crowd attendances, league placing, financial earnings – but Busby turned them down and took the job at Old Trafford instead. What he wanted was a chance to start from scratch, to build a team made up of players he had personally picked and trained. Furthermore, he wanted to be involved on every level of the club's activity, from the tea ladies right up to Head Coach, so that he was able to exert every power and influence over the building and maintenance of that team. This is precisely what he had been offered at Manchester United.

If this all sounds as if Busby was a megalomaniac for the sake of it, he wasn't. The opposite was very much the case. He craved and demanded such a degree of control over proceedings because, as a player, he had experienced the kind of management under which the player is treated coldly and impersonally, so that he never knew where he stood with the club. In his day, a player could be sacked at any time without any warning and with no rights whatsoever. Busby wanted to change that. Where managers he played under had engendered a critical atmosphere within the dressing room and a sense of uneasy competition between the players, Busby wanted always to encourage his players, even in defeat, and foster a sense of unity and harmony within the team. For Busby, it was the opposition who were the enemy, not the other players in your own team.

Whatever Busby's methods were exactly, they worked, and his record speaks for itself. He was Manager of Manchester United from1945 to1969 and then again, briefly, between 1970 and 1971. In that time, United were crowned League Champions in 1952, '56, '57, '65 and '67, won the FA Cup in 1948, when United beat Blackpool 4-2, and again in 1963 with a 3-1 win against Leicester City. The final against Blackpool is often considered one of the finest Cup Finals ever played. His crowning achievement as a football manager, however, came in 1968, when Manchester United beat Benfica 4-1 to win the European Cup, the first English side ever to do so.

In many ways, Busby was the first modern football manager and his methods ushered football management into the modern age. Before him, managers were hired or fired at the whim of the chairman, but Busby was the first to define the role of manager as the 'boss', no longer merely as a servant to the board of directors. Instead of treating the job only as a matter of turning up on a Saturday afternoon to give a pep talk to the club's star players before the game, Busby spent most days with his players, checking on their progress week in, week out. He operated an open-door policy and encouraged anyone to come to him if there was a problem. Miscommunication between players and the management in his own day had done untold damage to team morale and therefore to performance and he had learnt that, however unpleasant it may be for all concerned, airing grievances was better than letting them fester.

Busby's role as manager to his players extended much further than the football pitch. On their days off, Busby took the players to play golf on a course called Daveyhulme.

Golf was not that common in those days and was something of a specialist sport. Footballers tend to be good golfers, though, and the players enjoyed the days out. For a few days before a big match, Busby would often take the whole first team to the Norbreck Hydro Hotel in Blackpool. Just yards from the sea, the hotel was replete with spas, baths and massage rooms where the players could limber up and relax. In the evenings, Busby took them to the best shows in town, which the players went to dressed in blazers liveried with the club crest and new grey flannels.

Busby went to great lengths to make his young players feel like part of a large family. Those who were not from Manchester were put in lodging houses, living together as brothers would. Indeed, some of his younger players were so young that Busby had to sign legal papers as their guardian before they were allowed to travel to Manchester to join the club. So, in both a metaphorical and literal sense, Busby was their father and he made absolutely sure that he, and not the chairman or the board, was the only head of this particular family.

Although Busby treated his players with kindness and respect, he was always reserved with them, slightly distant. His outward appearance of calmness, however, could be very badly ruffled. In exchange for the glory that Busby knew his players would achieve under him, Busby demanded absolute obedience from them and if he didn't get this from a player, Busby had no compunction in isolating and removing him from the team. The other side to this kindly father figure was a man who could harbour grudges and who could act ruthlessly when necessary. Ultimately, though, Busby was a peacemaker, not a troublemaker.

His privacy was vital to him and he valued it above everything else. By all accounts, he was only ever completely himself when with his family. In the crowded, close-knit world of the miners' cottages in which he'd grown up, privacy was very hard to come by. In the day to day life of his childhood, virtually everything had been public – sleeping, washing, going to the toilet – and so it comes as no surprise that Busby wanted to maintain his distance from people as much as he possibly could. Privacy wasn't a luxury for Busby, it was a necessity.

Alexander Matthew Busby was born in Old Orbiston, a mining village near the town of Bellshill, in Lanarkshire, Scotland in May 1909. According to family legend, the doctor who delivered him said "a footballer has come into this house today". Busby was known as 'Mattha' by his family and grew up, the eldest of four children, in a warm family atmosphere. Both his parents were Irish Catholics who had come to Scotland looking for work. There were eight pits around Belshill, each of which had its own community of miners living in rows of cottages called Miners' Rows. A row had sixteen houses, each house containing two bedrooms upstairs, a kitchen and a living room downstairs. There was one communal toilet for each row.

Conditions in these villages and towns were often squalid, with people living box- like on top of one another, but most families were decent, hard-working people who maintained good relations with each other. Born out of need, Catholics and Protestants in and around Belshill worked peacefully side by side for the most part, but tensions erupted every so often, usually on a Saturday night after too much drink. The minority of Catholics were called 'Tims' by the Protestants, who in turn were labelled 'Blue Noses' by the Catholics. The sense of being in the minority, of seeking solidarity with others who shared his beliefs, was key to Busby the man and never left him.

When the First World War broke out, his father, Alexander, like many other Irish Catholics living in Scotland, had no qualms about joining the British Army. Unfortunately, however, this allegiance would cost him his life. In 1916, when Busby was just six years old, his father was killed by a German sniper's bullet at Arras. As if this loss wasn't bad enough, by the time the war had ended, all his uncles were dead, too. The death of his father thrust new responsibilities onto Busby and his childhood immediately lost some of its innocence and sense of joy. With his mother working at the pithead all day, Busby now had to return straight home from school to help look after his three sisters instead of going out with his friends to play football. Later on in life, Busby said it was around this time that he started to develop a protective instinct towards those around him more sensitive and vulnerable than himself.

His mother remarried when Busby was ten. Although he got on with his new stepfather, the young Busby was no longer the centre of attention he had once been. It was another event that taught Busby self-reliance. He continued to do well at school and, when he was 12, he was sent to a local Catholic college to continue his studies. It would be a drain on family resources, but Busby's mother had always been a strong believer in education as a means to betterment and so the sacrifice was made. He walked the five miles there and five back every day for three years. Busby was a diligent, hardworking pupil, though his teachers noted that he could be detached from the rest of his class. He was told he was good enough to become a teacher but, just as he was finishing his studies, his mother and stepfather told him of their intentions to emigrate to the US. Many widows from the village had left for America after the war and word had got back to Old Orbiston that life was better in America. Busby did not want to go, but his mother couldn't wait another three years until Busby had finished his studies – times were too hard. Despite doing well at school, Busby never had any real intention of becoming a teacher and so he told her, if it was a matter of money, he would work down the pit, which is exactly what he did. He left the college and got a job as a miner. The family stayed in Old Orbiston.

The town was known in the area as 'Cannibal Island' because of the passion with which its miners played football. As a boy, Busby had played football in the streets every day and, even then, showed strong leadership qualities, so much so that his grandfather nicknamed him 'Bryn boru', meaning 'leader of men'. Now that his schooling was over, Busby was able to concentrate on football, which was what he wanted to do more than anything else. Working all week down the mines, he joined the village football team and played every weekend. Busby's boyhood footballing hero was Alex James, who also came from Bellshill and who was one of the greatest inside-forwards the game has ever seen. As a teenager, James played for Old Orbiston Celtic at the same time that Busby was the team's 'hamper-boy', in charge of looking after the team's stockings, knickers and jerseys. Before every match, Busby would hand each player his strip. On one occasion, James's boots were mislaid and Busby ran the 200 yards to his family home and collected his own pair. They fitted James perfectly.

James went on to greater things, playing for Preston North End, Arsenal and Scotland in a long and glittering career. Two other well-known players, Jimmy McMullen and Hughie Gallacher, also came from Bellshill and news of the footballing exploits of all three during the early and mid-1920s spread pride and joy through the communities of Old Orbiston and Bellshill at a time when there was little else to shout about. The three of them were members of the 'Wee Wembley Wizards', the famous Scottish side that beat England 5-2 at Wembley in 1928, an event that absolutely captivated Busby's imagination and, more than any other single event, made him determined to succeed as a footballer.

Busby was improving all the time as a footballer and he moved from the village football side to Alpine Villa, the best youth team in the area. With Villa, Busby won the Scottish Under-18 Cup and the celebrations took place in Bellshill

Miners' Club. It was that night that Busby met and fell in love with Jean Menzies and they started courting straight away. He then moved from Alpine Villa to the junior club, Denny Hibs, thus following in his hero Alex James's footsteps. Within a couple of months of that move, however, he was spotted by Manchester City and asked if he wanted to sign professionally. He did, and signed his contract in the Bank restaurant in Glasgow. He left Bellshill, for good as it turned out, but promised Jean he would be back.

In his first season at City, he was put into the team at inside-left, the position in which Alex James had played, but Busby soon found out that he just didn't have the required pace. The manager tried him at outside-right and centre-forward, but this did nothing to improve his performances. The manager was patient, though – he knew it took time for new players to settle into new positions and new teams. There was nothing to do except wait and hope that Busby would come good in the end.

Despite his troubles on the pitch, Busby was well-liked at Maine Road by both players and management. Always smartly turned out, he seemed comfortable within himself, attending Mass regularly but also joining in the dressing room banter. Never drawing attention to himself, he wasn't an obvious target for the other players to make fun of, but they couldn't get to know him very well either. There was something intangible about him. He seemed much older than his 20 years and this maturity set him apart from the others.

His performances on field continued to be extremely disappointing and, after yet another dismal performance, he'd had enough. Packing his bags one Saturday evening he decided he would give up football altogether and return to his old mining job in Scotland. There was an overnight train to Glasgow that left Manchester every evening. But for a fortuitous intervention that evening, Busby would indeed have caught the night train and we might never have heard of him again.

At this time, Jimmy McMullen was the Manchester City captain and had taken Busby under his wing when Busby arrived at Maine Road. On this particular evening, McMullen happened to call on Busby just as Busby was packing his bags. McMullen sat him down and, over a bottle of whisky, talked to Busby all night. He told Busby not to leave, that he would regret it for the rest of his life if he did. He told Busby of his own experiences when he first joined the club and said that it always took a couple of years to settle down. Be patient, he said, don't give up. McMullen even invited Busby to come and room with him and his family until things got better for him.

It was a lovely gesture by McMullen, but it didn't quite work out the way he intended. Busby was patient and didn't give up, but he continued to perform well below par. After two seasons of frustration and depression at City, Busby reached an all-time low – he was dropped from the reserves, the ultimate indignity for a professional footballer. Watching City's third team play from the sidelines one Sunday, he was asked to fill in at right-half for a player who hadn't turned up. It was a position Busby had never played in before, but he was a revelation that day. As an inside-forward, Busby had always received the ball facing his own goal and never had the pace to turn and accelerate away from defenders. As a wing-half, however, he received the ball as he was running forward – his lack of pace mattered less and his shrewd passing game came into its own. Busby said later on that it was the first game in the whole of his first two seasons in England that he actually enjoyed playing. The following week he played right-half for the reserves and the week after that he was at right-half for the first team. Finally, Busby had arrived.

City reached the FA Cup Final in 1933 but lost 3-0 to Everton. The following year, they made it to the Final again, this time against Portsmouth. City's keeper that day was an unknown 19-year old called Frank Swift, whom Busby had, in turn, taken under his wing now that Busby had settled and was a more seasoned player. Swift had got his chance to play after the first and second choice keepers were injured. Early on in the game, Busby passed the ball back so that Swift could get a first-time touch on the ball. "I never forgot that wonderful gesture by Matt," Swift later said. The match was 1-1 until three minutes from time, at which point City scored and clinched a late win. So overcome by the occasion was Swift that, on hearing the final whistle, the youngster fainted and had to be revived to collect his medal from King George V. Busby was named Man of the Match. Indeed, 1934 turned out to be Busby's *annus mirabilis* – as well as his FA Cup Winner's medal, he won the first of his eight caps, playing for Scotland against Wales in the Home International series.

Things continued to go well for Busby until a hamstring injury two seasons later. The injury was quite bad and, although Busby responded to treatment, his recovery was slow, too slow for City, as it turned out. Busby was suddenly and unceremoniously sold to Liverpool. It was not an uncommon story. In those days, injured players were not treated at all well. They were left to fend for themselves and if they didn't mend quickly, they were callously sold on. City's ruthless attitude towards individuals like himself disgusted Busby. He said, "When I moved from Manchester City to Liverpool I vowed that if I ever became a manager I would respect players as individuals."

Ironically, and somewhat cruelly, Manchester City went on to win the First Division championship the season Busby was sold. After that, though, the club went into a sharp decline and were relegated from the top flight of football the season after they had been crowned champions. The change of fortune amazed everyone, including Busby, but after his treatment at the club, there was no sentimentality on his part. The lesson he learnt was that success was fleeting if the foundations on which it rests are flimsy. Build a solid family-like club atmosphere from the bottom up, he reasoned, and any success the club achieved would be shared by all and, most importantly, it would last longer.

Busby liked being at Liverpool and immediately fitted in. The set-up at Liverpool couldn't have been in starker contrast to that at City. Players were treated with kindness and consideration. Soon after Busby arrived, for instance, the 32-year old Jimmy McDougal, a veteran half-back with more than 350 appearances for the club to his name, was replaced by a younger player. McDougal, however, was immediately re-signed on top wages, even though he had lost his place in the first team. For the whole of the following season, much to Busby's astonishment, McDougal was paid full wages again despite not playing at all. At the end of that season, there was no option left open to McDougal other than to retire. The terms of his contract meant that, if he did retire, he would not qualify for a large 'benefit' payment he was due in six months' time, but the manager, George Kay, persuaded the directors to promise that he would receive the payment in any case. This act of generosity left a huge impression on Busby.

In all, Busby spent three seasons at Liverpool, a spell he enjoyed enormously despite not winning any major trophies. Busby's qualities as a man blossomed during his years at Liverpool. By now, he was no longer the unsettled 20-year old reserve but, at 30, was now the senior pro in the side, someone the younger players in the dressing-room looked up to. He treated everyone equally and with kindness and was the man they would go to if they had any problems. He was also very patient, taking the time to help younger players with their game, encouraging instead of lambasting them.

He was concerned for the plight of others, a sense of welfare that had developed from his childhood days in Bellshill. The other, younger players drew strength and courage from his presence and all who crossed paths with Busby commented on the calmness he exuded as a person.

When war was declared on 1st September 1939, the Football League was immediately suspended without further notice. All the Liverpool players enlisted for the Territorial Army, and Busby did the same. The War Office decided that professional sportsmen would best serve their country by acting as Physical Education instructors in order to keep the troops fit and healthy, therefore boosting morale. Busby's name was put forward and accepted as one of a number of suitable candidates for such a posting. He was sent to Aldershot where he became an NCO with the rank Company Sergeant-Major Instructor. The big football clubs still played informally from time to time and it was decided that professional players could 'guest' for whichever team was nearest to where they had been stationed. Naturally, Busby was keen to keep his hand in as a player and so, during his spell in the Army, he played for Reading and Aldershot as often as he could. He even earned six more 'unofficial' caps playing for his country.

After the Allies started the invasion of Italy in May 1943, Busby was sent with the Army's First XI to entertain the troops in the south of the country. Made Officer-in-Charge, he was responsible for the training and tactics of the team. It was Busby's first taste of management and he revelled in it, but he was soon back in Aldershot. And so the war dragged on is this way, neither stretching Busby in particular, nor boring him either. The war had lasted a lot longer than anyone could have predicted. Like many men whose peacetime lives had been interrupted by the war and then held in suspension until it was over, all Busby could do was wait. Then, in December 1944, Busby received a letter that was to change his life forever.

Louis Rocca, an old friend of Busby's who was on the board at Manchester United, wrote to Busby offering him the job of managing the club. Busby took stock of his situation. The war was coming to an end and Busby was 35 – too old to resume his playing career. He had enjoyed being in charge of the Army XI more than he imagined he would, especially enjoying the discipline required of managing a football team. He felt he could express himself. Busby wrote back saying that he was interested and would get back to him.

Somewhat serendipitously, Busby was then approached by Liverpool to become their manager. Being a popular and well-respected former player, Busby was an obvious choice for Liverpool, but Busby kept Liverpool waiting – he now had a bit of bargaining power in his negotiations with United and he wanted to see what he how far he could push things with them. In February 1945, he initiated a meeting with James Gibson, the chairman of Manchester United and, in no uncertain terms, Busby set down exactly how he wanted to run the club. He would be respectful of the board, he said, but he would not be at their behest. He demanded total control over all aspects of the players and ground staff. If he was going to be given the responsibility of managing the club, he insisted on being given the complete power to do so. Gibson balked at Busby's plain-spoken and direct terms, but he was impressed, too. Unbeknownst to Busby, Gibson actually shared Busby's vision and agreed with him on almost every point. Gibson knew immediately that Busby was the right man for the job and so, on 19th February, overseen by Walter Crickmer, Busby signed a five-year contract with Manchester United. Liverpool FC were less than pleased.

Sergeant-Major Busby was demobbed in October 1945. He and his wife, Jean, and their children Sheena and Sandy, moved into a house owned by the club in Chortle, two miles from Old Trafford. When Busby took over as manager, United were sixteenth in the Northern League (the Football League was still suspended) and for the previous two decades they had performed very poorly indeed.

In 1925, United had been newly promoted to Division One, but for the next few seasons, they remained on the verge of relegation. The depression in the '20s hit football hard, turning it into something of a luxury that few people could afford. And even if there was a team in Manchester worth watching, it was City, who were riding high in the First Division. Then, in 1927, disaster struck – John H Davies, United's chairman and the original benefactor who had come to the club's rescue in 1902, died, taking with him the financial safety net that he had provided for the club. Labelling himself 'Secretary-Manager', Walter Crickmer took over the running of the club until another chairman could be found.

By 1930, United were bottom of Division One and still without a chairman. A paltry 3,900 spectators attended the final match of that season against Middlesbrough, which ended in a 4-4 draw. It was not enough to save United from relegation, however, and it is the relegation that, to this day, remains the lowest point in the club's long and extremely distinguished history. The club was now in huge financial difficulties and on the brink of bankruptcy. The mortgage on Old Trafford, debts to creditors and banks as well as reduced attendances meant that, on Fridays, players were often left waiting in the dressing room until lunchtime while Crickmer went cap in hand to the bank to ask for the money to pay them their weekly wages.

Meanwhile, Louis Rocca was working hard to try to find new sources of investment. He met with all the city's wealthiest businessmen but, one by one, they turned him down. In spite of this, Rocca persevered and eventually found support from a local clothing manufacturer and retailer named James

Gibson who promised to make funds immediately available. However, Gibson was no sentimentalist. He made a public announcement that, unless United's supporters responded by attending matches, he would withdraw his financial support for the club. The next home fixture was a Second Division game against Wolverhampton Wanderers, which United narrowly won 3-2. The attendance that day was 33,312 – Gibson had his answer. After the match, Gibson held a press conference pledging his continued support.

The club continued on its rocky path. In 1936, United gained promotion to the First Division only to be relegated the same season. Their manager, Scott Duncan, resigned and Walter Crickmer once again found himself running the club as Secretary-Manager. In the following few months, Louis Rocca, acting as Chief Scout, signed in quick succession four players who would go on to become among the most celebrated names ever at United and among the most illustrious names in the history of the game: Johnny Carey, Jack Rowley, Stan Pearson and Allenby Chilton. In 1938, with the help of these players, United were promoted to the top flight once again.

Over his first few seasons, Gibson became more involved in the running and planning of the club. In order to avoid having to pay huge sums of money for new players, money that the club simply didn't have, one of Gibson's suggestions was to concentrate on youth policy and set up a system of junior teams at the club. To this end, the Manchester United Junior Athletic Club (MUJAC) was inaugurated in 1938 and the first crop of local lads were taken on. A group of teachers and instructors from the University of Manchester were recruited to help teach and train the youngsters, a move unheard of at the time. By 1939, the youth policy at Manchester United was well established and was already producing impressive results. In the Chorlton League, for example, the youth team scored 223 goals in one season.

At the last AGM before the outbreak of war, conditions at
the club looked better than they had done for years. Although
United only finished fourteenth in their first season back in
Division One, it was a much better placing than was expected.
The Reserves had just won the Central League, the junior 'A'
team had won their league and the boys at the MUJAC had
won their division of the Chorlton League. At the meeting,
Gibson said, "We have no intention of buying any more
mediocrities. In years to come we will have a Manchester
United composed of Manchester players."

Now that the war was over, everyone was eager to take up
where things had been left off. Gibson and the board expected
great things from Busby after his extraordinary 'call to arms'
speech to Gibson. They wanted a new era. Busby's first act
as Manager, however, was not to buy any new players, but to
appoint a man named Jimmy Murphy as Head Coach. Nobody
had ever heard of this Murphy. Who was he? Where had he
come from? Busby didn't know the man that well himself,
but he had played against him before the war, when Murphy
was playing for West Bromwich Albion and Busby was at
Manchester City. The circumstance surrounding the moment
they actually did meet is part of United folklore.

On one of his assignments to Italy during the war, Busby
was sent to Bari, on the heel of Italy, to a transit camp for
serviceman who had just defeated Rommel's Africa Korps
in North Africa. Whilst wandering around the camp, Busby
came across a man giving a talk to a group of soldiers before
a game of football. Something about the way this man was
talking to them made Busby stop and listen. The man was fiery,
passionate. He ranted and raved at them. There was nothing
riding on this game, it was just a friendly against another
army eleven, but the man was treating it like a Cup Final,
encouraging and pushing them to play better, to win. He just
wouldn't stop. The man was Jimmy Murphy.

Busby was impressed. In Murphy, Busby recognised something that he lacked – that directness and boldness with the players, the ability to get in amongst them and be one of them. In dealing with the players himself, Busby knew he was much calmer, more strategic, more aloof, and in Murphy, he saw someone who could help him achieve his long-term goals. "It was his attitude, his command, his enthusiasm and his whole driving, determined action and word power that caused me to say to myself, 'he's the man for me'", Busby later said. At the end of the game, he approached Murphy and began talking about his ideas for his future as a football manager. Murphy listened and understood immediately where Busby was coming from. Busby made and an offer of employment as coach – Murphy said yes straightaway. "It was," Busby said, "my first and greatest signing for Manchester United".

Murphy was Manchester United's Head Coach from 1945 to 1955 and Assistant Manager from 1955 to 1971. While Matt Busby was in hospital following the air crash in Munich, Murphy was Manager for six months, from February until August 1958. He was also Manager of Wales from 1956 to 1963 and took Wales to the World Cup Finals in 1958, where they reached the quarter-finals. It is the only time Wales have ever reached the Finals.

Harry Gregg describes Murphy as "a rough diamond, a beautiful diamond. Five eight, five nine. Stocky built without being heavy, not light, heavy smoker like me, didn't drive a car, went everywhere by taxi. Would be grinding his teeth a lot. Would be full of fire, full of passion, a smoker's voice, harsh voice, aye."

Bobby Charlton said of him: "Alf Ramsay helped me a lot, as did Matt Busby but Jimmy got to my guts: there have been few better teachers in the game. Whatever I achieved in football I owe to one man and only one man, Jimmy Murphy."

Nobby Stiles: "Jimmy Murphy was a nuts and bolts man, covering each and every detail. He taught me that the game was simple and taught me to play to my strengths. Jimmy was the power behind the throne."

James Patrick Murphy was born in October 1910 and raised in Pentre, a mining village in the Rhondda Valley in Glamorgan, Wales. In an uncannily similar story to Busby's parents in Scotland, Murphy's father, William, was an Irishman who had come to Rhondda from Kilkenny to look for work. Murphy's Welsh mother, Florence, was a widow with six children when she met William. They married and had Jimmy, their only child. While William was Catholic, Florence was Welsh Chapel and although Jimmy was brought up a Catholic in a largely Protestant household, there was no ill-feeling within the family. Like Busby, the men in Murphy's large family worked down the coal mines, including his four brothers. As a boy, Murphy used to play the organ in the local church and his mother wanted him to go into the music business, but Murphy was also a good footballer and decided to become a professional footballer instead. He played for Pentre Linnets and then Welsh Schoolboys, but he remained a beautiful piano player all his life and often played Mozart and Beethoven for the players during the post-match celebrations.

He signed for West Bromwich Albion when he was 17 but, like Busby, had a mixed time of it at his first professional club. He was very lonely in the early days, but ended up playing more than 200 games at left-back for West Brom, without ever scoring a single goal. His nickname was 'Tapper' because of his very hard tackling — it is said that some players had to wear two pairs of shin pads when they played against him. He reached the FA Cup Final with West Bromwich Albion the year after Busby won the Cup with Manchester City, but

West Brom lost 4-2 to Sheffield Wednesday. He won 22 caps as a Welsh International and captained his country on two occasions. Like so many other professional footballers, the war effectively ended his career.

He joined the Royal Artillery and was posted to North Africa. Put in charge of an anti-aircraft gun unit, he saw little action and never actually fired a shot against the enemy. All he did was organise and play in football matches. Towards the end of the war, as the Germans were driven north, so his regiment moved through Tunisia and Sicily and into southern Italy, which is when he met Busby and accepted Busby's offer of employment.

As Head Coach, Murphy was in charge of the Reserve team as well as scouting for, recruiting and coaching the youth teams – basically everything up to but excluding the First XI. On more than one occasion, he camped outside a potential signing's house to make sure he got their signature before anybody else. When he felt a reserve player was ready to play in the top-flight, he let Busby know and Busby, trusting Murphy implicitly, would invariably pick the player for the next available match. This is extraordinary by today's standards, where a player is put on as a substitute for the last ten minutes of a game several times before being given the nod to start. In Busby and Murphy's time, there were no substitutes, so a player either played from the beginning of the match or not at all.

Murphy worked from nine in the morning until late at night. He never drove a car and travelled to Old Trafford each day by taxi or train. He was always dressed in a suit and tie in winter, slacks and a blazer in summer. Before lunchtime, he would work with the Colts, Reserves and First XI, all of whom trained at Old Trafford, the afternoons were spent on remedial teaching. At six o'clock on Tuesdays and Thursdays, he arrived at United's training ground, called The Cliff, and spent the evening coaching the youth teams.

The young lads loved Murphy – he treated them like sons – but he would yell and scream at them if they did something he didn't like. It was all part of Murphy's method – he wanted the boy to bounce back the next week and fight his corner to prove Murphy wrong. If the boy had character, that's what he would do. All the boys in the youth teams had talent – it was what had got them to Manchester United in the first place – but to make it into the first team, they would have to have team spirit, determination and courage – in a word, character. As for the older players, well, they didn't like him at all because Murphy only encountered them when they had been dropped to the Reserves and all he ever did was swear at them.

Murphy was not a complicated coach. He taught a simple set of basic principles: the importance of passing; changing the point of attack; defending; getting the ball back by working hard as a team. The team was always more important than the individuals in it. Football is all about getting it and giving it. "Get the ball," he would say, "and give it to a red shirt."

Off the pitch, He often talked about football to players on a one-to-one basis for hours on end. He was evangelical about it, lived and breathed it, working seventy or eighty hours a week without recompense for the extra time he put in. But he did have some help, from a man named Bert Whalley, whom Busby signed in 1947 to assist Murphy with the youth and reserve teams. Whalley had played at left-half for United, making 33 first team appearances before an eye injury ended his career. Like many successful managers and coaches, Whalley was only ever an average player. He was a Methodist Lay Preacher (giving lie to the claim that United was a purely Catholic club), a teetotaller and the perfect foil for Murphy. They worked so closely together that they seemed like brothers, each finishing the other's sentence.

One of Murphy's jobs was to give the team talks just before the game on a Saturday. The team talk was always the same. With Whalley standing by, the first thing Murphy would do is tear up the opposition team-sheet. "Forget them," he would say, "they can't play. They're useless. See this red shirt, it's the best in the world, when you put that on nothing can beat you." Then, he would give each player a rundown of his opponent's strengths and weaknesses, effing and blinding all the way. The language he used was so bad that Bert Whalley had to leave the room. Famously, he always ended his pre-match talk by telling them to "go out and enjoy yourselves". At half time, regardless of the score, his advice was always the same: "Get bloody stuck in!"

Jimmy Murphy and Matt Busby couldn't have been more different as men and the only thing they had in common was football. But when matters did come down to football, Murphy never tried to usurp Busby's position and fully accepted his role as Busby's assistant. That didn't mean he didn't say what he felt – he would always offer his honest opinions during discussion but, having made his point, he accepted Busby's decision as final. Throughout his career, Murphy received several job offers to become Manager himself, from clubs including Arsenal, Juventus and even the Brazilian national team, but his loyalty remained with Manchester United. He considered the club to be his life's work.

For all his fire and brimstone, however, Murphy was ultimately a hugely affectionate and compassionate man and there is one story that shows this side of him better than any other. In the FA Youth Cup one year, Manchester United Colts were playing Nantwich in the Second Round. They won the game 23-0 and, understandably, the Nantwich keeper was in shock afterwards. Seeing how upset the boy was, Murphy went up to him and signed him up on the spot. He patted him on the back. "You can't be that bad," Murphy told him, "because you're a United player now."

★ ★ ★

Busby's first season as Manager, with Murphy as Head Coach at his side, was a frustrating one – most of the players Busby would have picked for the first team were still away in the armed forces and, with such limited resources, Busby had very few options. There was still no Football League to speak of and so, in order to help clubs make more money, the FA ruled that the FA Cup would now have two legs in every round right up to the semi-finals. This didn't help Manchester United at all, though, as they had a poor cup run and exited the competition early.

It wasn't until the 1946/47 season that United's star players like Stan Pearson, Jack Rowley and Allenby Chilton returned, and that the Football League proper resumed. Johnny Aston, a product of the fledgling MUJAC system, made his debut that season, too. With everything now in place, Busby's presence started to have a huge and galvanising effect on Manchester United. In just his second season as Manager, United's attendances had risen sharply and they finished second in the Championship – their best placing in years. United had fired Manchester's imagination once again.

The following season – 1947/48 – United again finished second in the Championship. In addition, they reached the FA Cup Final, playing against Blackpool. It was a thrilling game, by common consent one of the best Cup Finals ever, in which United came back from behind twice and clinched a 4-2 win on the day. Ten years old at the time, Bobby Charlton recalls that day: "We played for East Northumberland Boys in the morning and we were invited to go to one of the lads' houses to listen to the Cup Final on the radio. We had no television in those days. After a while we went out onto the street to play football – we couldn't get enough in one day – and every so often we would come in to ask the score.

I remember United equalising. The next we heard they'd won. They said it was the greatest Cup Final of all time. I think it was from that day that I wanted to be a footballer and join Manchester United."

Johnny Carey was named Footballer of the Year in the 1947/48 season and in 1949, United once again finished second in Division One. Despite the marked improvement, however, Busby knew the team that had won the Cup in '48 had already reached its peak. Most of the players were thirty years old or more. Add to this the fact that Murphy admitted to Busby that none of the young players coming through the reserves were good enough for the first team and Busby knew he had a problem. Not immediately, perhaps, but some time soon, Busby was going to have to find the players to make up the United of the future.

Given Busby's yearning for a new start, it was perhaps auspicious that the rebuilding at Old Trafford was finally finished and ready for the beginning of the 1949/50 season. Among those who watched United's first home game there – a 3-0 win over old rivals Bolton Wanderers – were three players in United's youth teams: 20-year-old Roger Byrne, 15-year-old Jackie Blanchflower, and 15-year-old Mark Jones. At the end of the season, Ray Wood was bought from Darlington for £6,000 to replace Jack Crompton, who had not performed well in goal all season. In the summer of 1951, Busby signed Johnny Berry from Birmingham City for the enormous sum of £25,000 after Charlie Mitten had defected and gone to play football in Columbia. The old guard was gradually being replaced by the new arrivals.

In November 1951, Roger Byrne and Jackie Blanchflower made their first-team debuts at Anfield against Liverpool. At the end of the 1951/52 season, somewhat unexpectedly, United won the Championship, but it wasn't among the greatest of Busby's achievements as manager since his team had not played that well all season. Rather, it was the last hurrah for the team of '48, the team who had played so brilliantly at Wembley to win the Cup. Jack Rowley, Johnny Carey, Allenby Chilton, Stan Pearson and Johnny Aston were all now feeling the heat from below, from the youth and reserve players who were not so much banging on the door as bashing it down to get a game in the first team. Deciding to bow out while the going was good, Johnny Carey, at United since 1937 and Busby's most loyal player, the very epitome of what Busby looked for in a player, retired at the end of the '51/52 season. The captaincy was given to the young gun, Roger Byrne.

2

YOUTH POLICY 1952-57

The 1950s was a gloomy time for Britain. The country had not yet recovered at all from the war. It was in chronic debt to the United States, had no economy to speak of and little food. Rationing was still in place and would remain so until 1954. The country was relentlessly monochrome, the drab winter landscapes of its cities perfectly captured in black-and-white Ealing films such as *Hue and Cry* and *Passport to Pimlico*. These films dealt with the struggles of the common man against a government who told him that, when he wasn't sleeping, he should be working harder. Prime Minister Clement Atlee embarked on grand scheme to nationalise the steel and coal industries "on behalf of the people", but the 'people' could not have cared less. They were sick of being told to work harder, sick of there being no food or money, sick of being cold or, in some cases, homeless.

The Festival of Britain, that magnificent folly, opened to a bewildered public in May 1951. Many complained that the extravagant sums needed to stage it could have been better spent building new houses for the poor and homeless, but

Deputy Prime Minister Herbert Morrison presented it as a "tonic for the nation", an attempt to put some pride back into post-war Britain in full view of the world's media. Whatever view you took, though, it was an extraordinary display of new structures, images and ideas, unabashedly forward-looking in concept and content.

Then, on 6th February 1952, King George VI died and his beautiful young daughter became Queen Elizabeth II. For the older generation, his death marked the symbolic passing of the war years. Elizabeth's coronation of 1953 was one of the first events to be shown on national television and, for that reason, it glued the nation together like few things had done before the advent of TV. Many felt that something youthful and new was initiated by Elizabeth's succession to the throne – for a lot of the younger generation, however, the coronation was greeted with nothing but indifference. For them, royalty had very little to do with the realities of 1950s Britain.

The youth of Britain was changing. No longer did they listen to Glenn Miller or Judy Garland as their parents had, they listened to Charlie Parker's bebop, Lonnie Donnegan's skiffle band – the punk music of its day – or Bill Haley & His Comets playing "Rock Around the Clock". Because there was so little money or opportunity for the youth to get hold of luxurious goods, young people invested a huge amount of significance into new music. It gave them an identity. Later on, in 1956, a song called "Heartbreak Hotel" started playing on the radio and everyone fell in love with Elvis Presley. Teddy boys, with their long-draped, velvet jackets and drainpipe trousers, began to appear everywhere. The word 'teenager', coined in America and exported to Britain after the war, was seized by the nation's youth and used as a badge of honour. An 'adolescent' was depressed and confused, but a 'teenager' was in control of his or her life and future. Youth culture was born.

In the world of sport, times were changing, too. In 1952, an English woman named Ann Davison became the first woman to cross the Atlantic single-handedly. In an expedition headed by an Englishman, Lord Hunt, mountaineers Edmund Hilary and Sherpa Tenzing conquered Everest in 1953, and in 1954, Roger Bannister ran the first 4-minute mile on an athletics track just outside Oxford. Sportsmen and women were pushing the limits of what could be achieved and, in an era with precious little to celebrate, became the heroes of the age.

In the late '40s and early '50s, however, football in England was much as it had been for years. Football boots had steel toecaps and were boots, not shoes. Players needed those steel toecaps, though, as the footballs in those days were made of heavy, laced-up leather and weighed as much as a bag of hammers. In that era, it was the gentlemanly Stanley Matthews, more than any other, who personified everything about English football. In 1953, his team, Blackpool, beat Bolton Wanderers 4-3 in a classic FA Cup Final, a game that became known as 'The Matthews Final'. At United, the captain Johnny Carey was known as 'Gentleman Carey', but many felt that the age of these modest older players, great though they indisputably were, had to draw to a close.

United's new captain, Roger Byrne, was altogether a different beast from Johnny Carey. Although Byrne and Busby didn't always see eye to eye off the pitch, watching him from the stands, Busby knew he had found his new captain in Byrne. He played with a strut that Carey didn't have, he respected opposing players yet also treated them with a scorn Carey lacked. It's been said that the only player Stanley Matthews ever got ruffled playing against was Roger Byrne. The young players had a confidence – cockiness even – that was alien to the war generation. The old ways and standards were fast disappearing and were being replaced by those of a newer generation, by players who looked forwards, not back, and who were encouraged by Busby to assert and express themselves in a way that the older, more self-deprecating generation would have found unseemly.

Although United's youth policy was actually initiated many years before Busby's appointment as manager, Busby put his faith in and staked his reputation on the idea of youth policy more than any other manager. He had, in fact, had the idea for a very long time indeed: "People often ask when I decided that the most important job was to attract and develop young players. The answer is that the importance of young players was at the back of my mind from the day I arrived at Manchester City as a youth player myself." This is another way in which Busby was a pioneer and a visionary.

The immediate post-war years saw a boom in attendance at football matches, but there was a dearth of good young players. This was yet another very good reason to set up a youth policy. Busby sought to recruit young lads just after leaving school in order to make and mould his own brand of player in whom a sense of family and loyalty would be instilled so that they would want to stay with the club. Busby tried to create a family atmosphere at the club, perhaps because of his own interrupted childhood, and this regeneration mirrored the country's own efforts to rebuild itself after the long, hard war years.

Busby used the foundations laid by Gibson as a platform from which to launch his own youth policy. He said, "I did not set out to build a team: the task ahead was much bigger than that. What I really embarked upon was the building of a system which would produce not one team but four or five, each occupying a rung of the ladder the summit of which was the First XI." In 1947, he had appointed Joe

Armstrong to work with Louis Rocca. Busby had played with Armstrong at Manchester City and the two had become friends. When Rocca died in 1950, Armstrong took over as Chief Scout and proceeded to set up an extremely well-developed scouting system at United in order to find the players to realise Busby's dream.

Before joining United, Armstrong used to work for the Post Office and knew how to operate quite complicated telephone exchange systems. He used these phone exchanges to keep in touch with the District Secretaries of the English Schools FA, finding out where and when the next games were being played. If there was any uncertainty about the exact location of these games, he had friends within the Post Office who would find a more accurate address for him. He also had a network of contacts in the local Manchester area, mainly schoolteachers with whom he kept in touch and who would tip him off about talented boys at their school. In this way, Armstrong made sure that a representative of the club, either himself or another scout, would be sure to attend every potentially significant schoolboy match in the whole of the north of England.

During the late 40s and early 50s, there were eight scouts employed by the club, three of whom operated in Northern Ireland. Armstrong sent these scouts around the country to attend the finals of inter-school competitions or local league finals. Sometimes, if Armstrong had a lead or a tip off, he would instruct the scouts to watch certain matches and report to him only about particular boys. Armstrong had a phenomenal memory and he kept records on every schoolboy he watched as well as assimilating the comments of other scouts into his records.

Armstrong and his scouts would then watch these players a few more times before making a final recommendation to one of the senior members of staff, usually either Jimmy

Murphy or Bert Whalley, who would then watch them before a decision was made whether or not to sign them. Jimmy Murphy apparently watched Tommy Taylor seventeen times before finally deciding to sign him. The offer would usually be made to the boy's family as soon as he left school, catching him early and so avoiding any expensive transfer fees the club would probably incur if they left it any longer. Joe Armstrong was well-known for targeting the mothers, wooing them with chocolates and flowers and, if they were Catholics, with a Miraculous Medal from a batch he'd bought on a trip to Rome. He was exceedingly charming with them and vaguely flirtatious, but in the way of an overbearing uncle – paternal, not at all threatening. Armstrong proved absolutely indispensable to Busby, who labelled him a "gentleman ferret".

Here is Albert Scanlon on the events surrounding his own recruitment to United: "And there was about thirty of us [boys playing football] and this chap come on and he was very regimental, and he says, 'I am looking for the boy Scanlon'. And nobody moved. Nobody said a word and they just looked at him. And he says, 'I'm Mr Whetton from St Margaret's Central High School and I need to speak to the boy Scanlon'. Nobody said a word, not a word, 'cos you was told, you don't speak to strangers. And then he looked round and he says, 'You're him'. So I said, 'Yes.' He says, 'Have you got a birth certificate?' And I said, 'Well I haven't, I suppose my mam has'. 'Well where's your mum?' I said, 'She's at work'. 'Where's your dad?' 'At work.' 'We will now go and get your birth certificate' he says. So Ted Whetton and thirty boys walked the Stretford Road to the Registrar's. And we got this birth certificate and he says, 'Right' he says, 'You will go home and tell your mother and father that you have been selected for Manchester Boys. You will be at the Queen Victoria monument in Piccadilly at three o'clock on Wednesday afternoon. You will bring boots, shin pads, towel.' So I told me mam and dad. Anyway, I played five games: Bolton, two against Liverpool, two against – six games – two against Swansea and one against Yorkshire and I scored four or five goals. And then we'd play football for schools and the first match was against Cheshire, I think, Cheshire at Rochdale. And as I say, we all travelled by bus, nobody had cars or anything. And on this bus was myself, my mum, my dad and my uncle John and we'd just beat Cheshire four three and I'd scored three and this little old fellow got up off the back seat, we're on the main road travelling down, and he went, 'Ladies and gentlemen, I want you to give a round of applause to this lad here who's just beaten Cheshire four three this morning.' It was Joe Armstrong, the scout at United, he was only a little fellow and they was all clapping. And about a week later I went in and there was this fellow sat in the chair talking with mam and dad. Me mam says, 'This is Mr Murphy from Old Trafford' and he says, 'We think we can make you a footballer'. He says, 'We can't guarantee it, but we think we can' and he says, 'I'm only gonna ask you once, when you leave school, would you care to sign for Manchester United?' I said, 'Yes, love it'. And he stood up, he shook my hand and he says, 'Right, you can go out and play now'."

By the time Bobby Charlton played for England Boys, he had already been snapped up by Armstrong, who saw Charlton play for East Northumberland Boys against Hebburn & Jarrow Boys some months earlier. Armstrong had been tipped off about him by Charlton's headmaster who was a former teacher at Manchester Grammar School and who had been on Armstrong's list of contacts. As soon as Armstrong clapped eyes on Charlton, he knew he had to act quickly, and he made a beeline for Bobby Charlton's mother ten minutes into the match and made an offer there and then. As well as Charlton, Armstrong also unearthed Duncan Edwards and David Pegg before they went on to play for England Boys. Everyone knew that Edwards was the outstanding schoolboy

talent in the country and competition was so fierce to secure
Edwards' signature that Bert Whalley had to drive Jimmy
Murphy late one night from Manchester to Edwards' family
home in Dudley, where Edwards had to be dragged out of
bed to sign the contract.

Whilst at the club, there was a hierarchy of teams that the
young players worked their way up:

FIRST XI
Official 'A' team (Reserves) – 17-18 onwards
Official 'B' team (Colts) – 17-18
Junior 'A' team – from 16-17
Junior 'B' team – from 15-16

Players started playing for the Junior 'B' team but, if they were
any good, and they usually were, they were quickly promoted
to the Junior 'A' team, which played in the Lancashire County
League. Players of exceptional talent, however, like all the
Busby Babes, shot through the ranks quickly and were usually
playing first-team football at 17, or soon after. Many of the
Babes really were babes when they made their first-team
debuts. Busby was no respecter of age, once famously saying
that "If they're good enough, they're old enough."

The junior teams travelled to games by corporation bus –
cars were few and far between in those days. A plush luxury
coach was used only for the Reserves and the First Team.
Albert Scanlon says, "We would meet on the left-hand side of
the door at the Grand Hotel, on the right of the door would
be the Colts. Round the corner was a coach laid on for the
First Team. They got ten bob, we got half a crown." The quality
of some of the pitches they played on was appalling. Albert
Scanlon remembers once playing on a pig farm in Burnage,
on the outskirts of Stockport.

The local and county leagues operated an 'open-age' football policy, so that these 15-year-old boys played against opponents of any age. It was often the case that the players in these leagues were five, ten or even fifteen years older than the boys. Sometimes the opposition would look at the Busby Babes and ask Jimmy Murphy 'When's the first team coming?' This was physically very hard on the boys, especially when they played the dockers, or the local factory teams such as Avros, Ferranti and Miles Platting. The hardened men in these teams wanted nothing more than to beat Manchester United Colts, or even the even younger A or B team, and would kick the youngsters off the pitch. But Busby knew what he was doing – he knew that, because the boys lacked the physical strength to match their opponents, they would be forced to make up for it in other areas: ability, teamwork and discipline.

Here's Albert Scanlon on one such occasion: "I think I was seventeen, and I was picked to play in the friendly at Lincoln and the right back was retiring age, in his thirties. And this ball come across, and this fellow was about six foot four, and it came on the edge of the box and I come in and I hit it and it flew in the net, but as I hit it, he hit me so they're bringing me round and Roger [Byrne]'s there, the captain, and he says to this fellow, 'It's a friendly, what did you do that for?' He says, 'It's these kids' he says, 'look at 'em', 'they should be still at school' he says, 'they shouldn't be playing professional football.'"

Although the games were physically hard, they were a marvellous education and gave the boys an opportunity to develop their skills. Games often ended in high scores for the junior teams: 18-0 or 20-0 was not unheard of. Scorelines like this instilled huge confidence in the boys as they were allowed, encouraged even, to explore their talent and express themselves fully.

Just before one game, Albert Scanlon remembers that "this fellow walked up and he'd got a trilby on and he said, 'Excuse me Mr Murphy,' he says, 'I challenged your reserve side, but these are young lads, d'you want me to tell our lads to take it easy?'. 'No, no' Jimmy says, 'tell your lads to play the normal game'. And this team hadn't been beaten for four years and we were winning ten none at halftime and he went mad Murphy, he went potty. And I think it finished thirty something none, and we're all in the big bath after the game and this chap walks past and he stops and he looks, and he takes his hat off and he says, 'Gentlemen, today I just retired from football management'. He threw his cap in the air and it landed in the bath and he walked out and that was it. He was in shock because he'd not seen young sixteen-year-olds and seventeen-year-olds do this to anybody else, never mind his team that had not been beaten for three, four years and we annihilated 'em."

The great Hungarian National team of the '50s used to prepare for big matches by playing against far inferior opponents whom they would beat by huge scores, thus building confidence. Like many other managers and coaches, Busby had watched that day in November 1953 when Hungary, in their cherry-red shirts and led out by a short, portly army major named Ferenc Puskás, beat England 6-3 at Wembley, the first foreign team ever to do so. This was the moment in post-war English football that changed everything. Albert Scanlon remembers watching the game, too. He had joined Bobby Charlton, Dave Pegg, Tommy Taylor, Jackie Blanchflower, Mark Jones and Billy Whelan at Mrs Watson's to watch the second half, the only half that was shown, on her television. Scanlon remembers the half time score – 4-2 to Hungary – coming as a real shock to the system. By the time the final whistle went, they could hardly believe what they'd seen.

The unthinkable had happened – the great Stanley Matthews, Billy Wright, et al had been soundly thrashed in the world's most famous football stadium. Billy Wright remembered walking out onto the pitch and seeing that the

Hungarians wore V-neck shirts with no collars and had on slipper-like boots that were cut below the ankle bone. He joked with Stan Mortenson that they would be no problem because they didn't even have the right kit. Totally underestimating the Hungarians and wholly unprepared for their style of play, the result shocked the nation and the game still ranks as one of the most famous games in history.

In the '50s, English football was all about knocking it back until there was an opportunity to boot the long ball up to the big centre-forward. Teams in those days were modelled on what is known as the 'WM' formation. The defence, right-back (no.2), centre-half (5) and left-back (3), occupied the three tips of the W, while the right-half (no.4) and left-half (no.6) occupied the lower points of the letter. Just in front of them, the inside-right (8) and inside-left (10) were positioned at the tips of the M, while the attack, consisting of right-wing (7), centre-forward (9) and left-wing (11), made up the letter's lower points.

The way the Hungarians played that day was in complete contrast to this fixed model. The Hungarians were highly mobile and kept on switching positions: their wingers swapped places frequently, full-backs became wingers and the forwards helped to defend. They were constantly on the move, forever making quick, decisive passes to each other, short passes so that they kept possession. In this way, whenever a player got the ball, he had about three options to pass it on. This level of mobility and possession play had never been seen before, setting off complete confusion and indecision amongst the English players and ripping the English team apart.

The second aspect of the Hungarians' play that totally bewitched England was the fact that they didn't play with a lone striker up front. Their number 9, Nándor Hidegkuti, played deep, as part of the midfield, which meant that the centre-half marking him was constantly pulled out of position.

Hidegkuti's role was to create opportunities for the two front men, Puskás and Sándor Kocsis, as well as acting as a striker himself – indeed, Hidegkuti scored a hat trick. Because Kocsis and Puskás wore the number 8 and 10 shirts respectively, the English assumed they were inside-forwards and so their positioning as strikers confused the English defence. This three-pronged form of attack had never been seen before. It made the Hungarians unpredictable because they could burst from their deep position at any time and score in any number of ways. The English defence was completely outfoxed that day, they simply had no answer to each Hungarian player's speed, accuracy and understanding with each other.

It was a footballing masterclass, beautiful to watch, but most of all, it exposed comprehensively the inherent and deep-seated unattractiveness of the English game. The new laws governing the offside rule introduced in 1926 had resulted in a 'safety first' attitude amongst football managers and coaches, an attitude that had inevitably led to an emphasis on the physical aspect of the game. Rather than allowing players to express their artistry, self-expression and skill, managers and coaches instructed their players to bring the opposition down if they got too hot to handle. Many argued, not least the Hungarians, that the English game had been in decline ever since. The Hungarian goalkeeper, Gyula Grosics, said after the game: "I feel that the English were very reluctant to give up a tradition of a game which was actually their invention and which had brought them so much success." The press went wild in their praise of the 'Magnificent Magyars' and the Great Debate about the future of English football began. The Guardian reported that the Hungarians had "reinvented football". Others commented that the 'safety first' approach to the English game had been shown to be a "false god" by the Hungarians. "Good football cannot thrive, cannot begin to flourish without imagination", one paper said.

The game had a profound effect on Busby, because the way the Hungarians played was exactly the style of play he was trying to instil into his young squad every Tuesday and Thursday evening on the Cliff. This was a 'new way' of playing, one that involved a high level of team play but also encouraged individuals to express themselves and not be afraid to show off their skills. Busby wanted his young players to play the 'beautiful game'.

During their time at the club, and especially between the ages of 15 and 17, Busby regarded the well-being of the boys as his full responsibility. This meant that he became like a second father to most of the boys; indeed, when Jackie Blanchflower arrived at the club from Northern Ireland aged just 16, Northern Irish regulations meant that he had to have a guardian. Busby duly signed the necessary documents. Busby knew that the years between 15 and 17 were crucial because what happened during this time would largely determine the boys' future. The law at the time meant that no football club could sign a boy until after he'd left school at 15 and it couldn't pay the boy professionally until he was 17. When a boy was signed by the club, it was as an amateur and he only received expenses.

Busby was well aware that not every boy would go on to sign professionally for the club, so he made sure that the club found them a job or put them on courses or apprenticeships to learn a trade so that they could support themselves if things didn't work out for them as footballers. Through this system, for example, Duncan Edwards became a joiner, Bill Foulkes was a collier and Jackie Blanchflower trained as a plumber. Some even carried on their education. When he joined United, Bobby Charlton enrolled at Stretford Grammar School to finish his O Levels, but the combined pressure of

schoolwork, playing two football matches at the weekend –
one on Saturday for his school and one on Sunday for the
United junior team – as well as training two evenings a week
meant that he left school and eventually took a job with an
engineering firm for £2 a week.

The other option for the boys during these two years was
to take a job as one of the groundstaff. This involved during
various manual jobs at the ground for which you received a
salary. Many of the boys preferred this as it was the next best
thing to playing professionally for the club. During his time as
a junior, Albert Scanlon chose to work at the ground. About
his first day at Old Trafford, Scanlon says: "There was only Bill
Inglis there. He was second team trainer. The first team, the
squad, was in America, they'd just won a championship [in
1952]. And Bill says, 'Go and have a walk round the ground'
and I walked round, there were two painters and they were
painting the girders red and one of them stood up, he said,
'Are you new?' and I said, 'Yeah'. And he says, 'Go and get us
a sky hook' and I went off. I said to Bill, 'I can't find this sky
hook' and he said, 'They're taking the Michael out of you' he
said, 'there's no such thing as a sky hook.'"

Scanlon continues: "And they give me a paintbrush and
they said, 'Just go and paint anything white' you know what
I mean, or something like that. And you used to get your
orders off Bill Inglis every morning and I had a gym to do, it
was massive, outside the ground, but there was no air, there
was no windows or nothing, just a little door and they had
a little room, the physiotherapy room, and it had three big
mats in, two big medicine balls, some weights and I had to
sweep that out and it was dust, all, rotten and then I had to get
buckets of water and then Bill'd come and inspect it and he'd
say, 'Go and get a shower now, you're finished'. And that was
my job for a hell of a long time, this bloody big gym. Every
Wednesday I used to have to dubbin all the boots, you know,

and I'd get half a crown off the reserves and five shilling off the first team, and I'd finish up more than I had with wages, but that was it all day, I was just covered in dirt."

In order to nurture the sense that the club was an extended 'family', Busby made sure the boys were all properly housed and well cared for. The club vetted and employed a group of landladies to run several boarding houses and lodgings in which the boys would stay together until they signed as professionals on the advent of their seventeenth birthdays. Most of these ladies had connections with the club going back as many as twenty years. The most famous of these landladies was Mrs Watson, who ran a boarding house at 5 Birch Avenue, Stretford, and who was also a tea lady at Old Trafford. Kenny Morgans remembers that it was "just a house and if they wanted to do our washing they charged us two and six and if they watched television they'd just charge us two and six". Breakfast was egg and bacon and dinner was at 5 o'clock sharp. All baths were taken at the ground. At one time or another, Kenny Morgans, Mark Jones, Bobby Charlton, Bill Whelan, Duncan Edwards, Tommy Taylor and Dave Pegg all resided with Mrs Watson.

At weekends, the boys whose families lived far away would occasionally return home, but if they were alone in Manchester for the weekend, Bert Whalley would invite them round to his house for afternoon tea. He served them tomatoes and ham salad, then took them to Sunday Service. And when the boys left the club to do their National Service, Bert Whalley used to write to them once a week, filling them in on what had happened at the club that week. Even while players were temporarily in the Army, the club ethos was maintained in the boys' lives.

Once you signed as a professional, however, it wasn't possible for you to lodge with Mrs Watson anymore, so the players found their own lodgings, often just a few doors away.

But even though the newly professional first team players would see the amateur juniors in the street all the time, the juniors were so in awe of them that they would not say a word to them. When he was a junior at United, Kenny Morgans lived just a few doors down from Tommy Taylor and he remembers that, even though he often found himself walking to Old Trafford at the same time as him, he made sure to walk a distance from Taylor.

Once their work and board were sorted out, Busby's biggest worry concerning the boys' welfare became what they would get up to in their own time when they weren't under his watchful eye. He issued a set of *Training Rules and Instructions*, which heavily recommended cutting down on smoking and cutting out drinking altogether. He warned them at every opportunity about the perils of drinking but, as long as there was no trouble, Busby had little choice but to let them loose when they needed it.

On Saturday nights, the first team players and reserves would usually meet at nine o'clock at the Locarno, a club in Sale, or they would go to a jazz club called the Bodega. Best friends Tommy Taylor and Jackie Blanchflower often went to the dogs at Belle Vue, or to a dark, packed nightclub called the Continental. Bobby Charlton and Duncan Edwards would sometimes accompany them, but they weren't old enough to drink. That didn't stop Taylor and Blanchflower, however.

On Tuesdays and Sundays, the players used to go to the Plaza Ballroom or the Cromford, which was owned by an ex-United player, Paddy McGrath. Jimmy Saville, then a young 'disc-jockey', was the Assistant Manager of the Plaza at the time. He remembers that the ladies used to call the players the 'ten tall men' and that they were always on their best behaviour. These places were the only form of entertainment the players had all week and were very popular, so much so that Roger Byrne held his wedding reception at the Cromford.

In order to encourage potentially less 'harmful' ways to pass the time, Busby had arranged with the managers of the Odeon, Royal and Gaiety cinemas in town to let the players in for free. The boys at Mrs Watson's went to the pictures every Friday night. Mark Jones would go through the evening paper and pick a film and, after their dinner of fish and chips, off they would go. When they arrived back, there was a bowl of cornflakes and milk waiting for each of them.

One Friday night, David Pegg and some other of the players staying at Mrs Watson's missed the last bus home. They ran as fast as they could all the way back but when they finally arrived home, Jimmy Murphy had already been tipped off and was there to give them a scolding for being so late in. Of course, Busby and Murphy couldn't stop every breach of discipline, but when there was a breach, it was taken care of with a warning rather than any stiff penalty. The players quickly learnt to cover for each other and hide any misdemeanours from Busby, which Busby knew all worked towards building a strong team spirit.

But even though the players covered for each other's misdemeanours, they couldn't quite escape Busby's ever-vigilant eye since there were pairs of eyes working for him all over the city. If a few of the players had been out drinking on a Saturday night, Busby would call a meeting and he say, "You, you, you and you were out Saturday night in this pub. You wasn't only drunk, you were fighting". No matter where the players went in Manchester, they were so famous that there was always someone waiting to phone Matt Busby and tell him what they had been up to.

Of course, Busby wanted nothing more than to see players never giving up on the pitch – battling till the bitter end was a sign of real character, but Busby defined 'character' as much in terms of how his players conducted themselves at every other time of the week as they did on a Saturday afternoon.

How they performed in training, how they spent their spare time, how they treated each other – these were the signs of real character for Busby.

Just as Busby oversaw as many aspects of the players' lives as he could, so he oversaw all aspects of their training. Indeed, so involved was he that he changed into a tracksuit and joined them for the daily training sessions. This might not sound so unusual to us now, but in those days, this was unheard of and quickly became known as 'tracksuit management'. Usually, players only ever saw managers on match days when, dressed in their Sunday best, they would deign to visit the dressing-room for a few minutes before the game. But his hands-on approach typified how different Busby was in his managerial style – he was a new breed of manager and was the first manager to join in training sessions in this way.

Back in 1949, Busby knew that his first great team had peaked in terms of what they could achieve, and he knew that he would have to find a new set of players to build another great team. Looking around the pitch during training sessions in 1953, it seemed to Busby that he had managed to do that successfully. He had depth and breadth in his squad of young and not-so-young players. Busby's absolute trust in United's scouting system, which is exactly why he wished to be involved in its set-up from the very beginning, had paid off handsomely. When a young player was brought to the club by Joe Armstrong, Bert Whalley or Jimmy Murphy, Busby knew that, if the scouts had done their job properly, which they nearly always did, the player would already have enough natural ability to be able to play at the highest level. Once recruited to the club, one of Busby's masterstrokes as a manager was the absolute faith he placed in his players. He never questioned their ability and showed them a respect that no manager before him had shown to players. No, the question of ability was a *fait accompli* – the real question was: how best to allow that talent to materialise and develop?

Busby believed that, if a player had natural ability, it should not be tampered with in any way, but rather, the best possible conditions should be set up to allow that ability to emerge and flourish to its fullest potential. This is exactly what Busby did. In training, Busby wanted his players to continue to explore their innate talents and express themselves as fully as possible. He wanted the players to become 'masters' of their own talent. He couldn't 'tell' a player to play well, he could only set up the right conditions for a player to play his own game and hope that he did so. The term 'mastery' implies something that can actually be taught, which in football translated into how well the players interacted with each other. This, in turn, could be broken down into things that could be practised on the training field, things like how they moved, how quickly they passed and how well they worked as a team.

Up until Matt Busby and Jimmy Murphy's tenure at United, standard training sessions involved the players walking around the pitch and then running around it. Working with a football during training was relatively rare. The common thinking was that if a player didn't see the ball during the week he would be 'hungry' for it on Saturday. Busby believed that this attitude was nonsense. He believed that the more the players practiced during the week, the more effortlessly they would reproduce it on the Saturday. The passing game would be such a second nature to them that they would play the same way regardless of who they met and completely without match-day nerves. This was the very opposite of how most managers of the day operated and Busby was years ahead of his time.

To warm up, the players would lap the pitch four times and end with a six sprints from one side of the pitch to the other. After the players had warmed up, Jimmy Murphy and

Bert Whalley would make the players practice passing and moving with the ball. Full-backs were taught to give the ball to wingers, who would then feed it to the inside-forwards. If the full-back got the ball passed back to him by the inside-forward, he should look for a change of play, by giving it to a wing-half, for instance. Once the ball is passed up to the wingers, the centre-forward should already have made a run into the box to receive the cross into the area, and so on. Murphy in particular was a stickler for his players passing the ball with the right amount of accuracy and weight. Scanlon says, "Matt Busby was suave but Jimmy would spit at you when he was talking, effing and blinding at you. And to Bert, he was another great coach, he'd say, 'Is that right Bert?' and he'd say, 'You're right Jim'."

They would then go through technical exercises for heading the ball. Kenny Morgans can remember one such exercise, which involved "running, running up and down the stand and they used to have a football tied to one of the tops of the stand, which was about nine foot high, so there'd be about twelve or thirteen of you running around and then you'd come up to this ball and you'd jump up and head the football… on a Saturday, when you jumped to head the ball, he [Murphy] used to tell you not to just jump and hope that you got the ball, but to jump up and get the ball and head it to one of your players." The team was well known for the number of players who could head the ball properly, with intention and direction rather than merely as a means of getting it away from danger. Mark Jones, Jackie Blanchflower and Tommy Taylor, in particular, were superb in the air.

Busby used shadow play extensively. He would make his players strip and change into full kit, then play against nobody, always passing and moving, getting it back and laying it off and moving again. He often said that football was a simple game, only made complicated or difficult by bad players and bad coaches. "The ball is made round to go round," he would say, "keep the ball flowing. Give it to a red shirt." The players always had to end with a shot on goal and then they'd start again. When asked why he made his players do this, Busby explained that if the players passed and moved enough during the week, they'd all know where their team mates were going to be without thinking on a Saturday afternoon. When the media found out that the Brazilians played shadow football it was thought to be revolutionary, but Busby had been doing it at Old Trafford for years.

Training was also remedial. If there had been a particular problem during the previous match, Murphy would take the player or players concerned and spend hours recreating the situation in order to rectify the problem. Busby and Murphy also wanted to ensure that they broke any bad habits the players may have picked displayed during matches. On one occasion, Murphy was training with Bobby Charlton and Wilf McGuinness, showing them a particular way of passing the ball. He told them to go round the back of the ground and practise passing the ball to one another in that particular fashion. Murphy then went home, had his tea and came back hours later, when it was night time. He went round to the back of the ground and found Charlton and McGuinness still hard at it.

Murphy worked particularly closely with Bobby Charlton. Everything that Charlton had learnt as a schoolboy player was considered a flaw by Murphy. At school, Charlton had prided himself on being able to kick the ball forty or fifty yards up the pitch, but Murphy pointed out that, by kicking it so far into the other half, all he had succeeded in doing was putting all his team mates around him out of the game. When he wasn't kicking the ball up field, Charlton liked to hang on to it and dribble. As soon as he received the ball, Murphy said, he should pass it to another player. "Keep it simple," he said, "give it to a red shirt." This went against Charlton's natural instincts and Murphy spent hours on the training ground bashing these bad habits out of him.

"I seen Jimmy Murphy with Bobby Charlton, whom he loved," Harry Gregg says, "And I saw him say on a Monday morning repeatedly – 'Bobby'. 'Yes Jimmy?' 'Bobby, you looked great on Saturday', that's when had hair, blond hair. 'Yes Jimmy.' 'Beautiful forty yard balls you hit, effing glory balls'. 'What do you mean Jimmy?' 'I'll tell you what' he said, 'you looked great, your feet off the fucking ground and your blond hair flowing and the crowd cheering. Glory balls'. He said, 'The crowd loved it and so did their bloody right back, you bloody clown. Two balls is better than one – you play one short, you draw him in, you get it back, he's out and you put it there, but you're playing bloody glory balls, you look beautiful and their bloody team think you're beautiful as well'." Murphy was certainly the making of Charlton, getting him to cut out the 'glory balls' and long dribbles and concentrate on short, one-touch passing instead. Charlton himself said Murphy "made me a professional."

Jimmy Murphy was Busby's mouthpiece on the training ground and his instructions were followed to the letter by the players. He agreed with every aspect of Busby's methods of training. Like Busby, he believed that if you took care of the basics, the innate talent would emerge, develop and improve. You couldn't make a player great if there wasn't talent there in the first place, and if there was talent there, a player wouldn't improve by teaching him how to do difficult things. If he was good enough, he should be able to do the difficult things anyway – what he needed to learn was the basics.

The principles that Murphy lived by were ones that he taught to all his players down the years, not just to the Busby Babes. When Murphy was going through the same training process with Nobby Stiles, he asked the person standing next to him what he thought of Stiles and they replied, "Good, Jimmy, very good. But whenever he gets the ball he makes a really simple pass." Murphy nodded and said, "Yeah, it took me three years to get Bobby Charlton to do that."

Tom Curry, a Geordie nicknamed 'Tosher' and considered by Busby to be "the best trainer in Britain", and Bill Inglis, a Woodbine forever hanging out his mouth, together ran the United dressing-rooms at Old Trafford and the Cliff. Both were always dressed in ankle-length white coats and did everything from laying out the kit for training, filling the baths, rubbing liniment into the players' legs and bandaging wounds. But there was another, very particular job they performed. Albert Scanlon explains:

"The dressing room's a very special place at United, there was the first team dressing room which was players that were regulars in the first team and they were all players that had come back after the war. They'd one or two they'd signed – they didn't sign many players, United. The other dressing room was chaotic, because it was big, but there were three times as many people in it and they had the same thing; huge bath, small baths, showers, but if the players wanted to do their hair – in them days, everybody put something on their hair, they had to be smart when they went out. So there was a jar of Brylcreem, a bottle of olive oil and a tub of Vaseline and you had your choice. So some people'd come in and use the Brylcreem and all, but they all come in and there was a little mirror and they'd all stand in front of that mirror. And that was there every day of the week, every week of the year. Bill and Tom just filled 'em up, just kept filling 'em up."

The influence these two men exerted on the players was, in a way, even greater than that of Busby or Murphy. They were not particularly adept trainers but they were close to

the lads, and looked after their every need. Albert Scanlon
says that, whenever United played an away match and were
staying in a hotel the night before, Tom Curry used to stay up
in reception until the last boy had come in after the night out.
But they also employed crafty tactics of their own to get the
best out of their charges. "I'm only a kid, seventeen, eighteen,"
Albert Scanlon says, "and I'm coming down the cinder track
and you might have to do – not all at once – you might have
to do ten laps round this football pitch and Bill'd drop in at
the side here, still with his cigarette in his left hand, and he'd
say, 'You can get David Pegg out of this side. You could be a
better player than him' and, you know, things like that. And
then about five minutes later he'd be going round with David
and he'd say to David, 'I've just been talking to that Scanlon
and he says we're gonna get you out of this first team'."

In five weeks of pre-season training, the players had three or
four practice matches a week, many more than any other club.
Busby and Murphy would play on opposite sides to inject some
needle into the games. Just before the season actually started,
there was always a practice match at Old Trafford open to the
public. The teams would be the first team defence and the
reserve attack against the first team attack and reserve defence.

If a player's build wasn't strong enough, he was given cod
liver oil and malt every morning. On match days, the players
used to have egg on toast and then a steak – no vegetables,
just the steak and then, just before the game, Busby used to
hand each player a little drop of sherry, which, they say, used
to prevent wind. Busby tried as hard as he could to bring
into his coaching techniques as much academic and medical
information as possible, however small. This was absolutely
unheard of at the time, although, it has to be said, Busby
made sure the team medic carried in his bag several packets
of Rothmans cigarettes, to be handed out after the game to
all the players who smoked.

After the Saturday match, the players would get into the communal bath, to which soda crystals had been added as a muscle relaxant. They had to stay in the bath for at least twenty minutes, after which they washed all the muck off in a shower and then they would have a soft soap massage. According to Albert Scanlon, Tom Curry would "give you what he'd call his soft soap bath and there was this big drum of soft soap and he'd just scoop it up and put it in the small bath, and he'd get all these bubbles and then he'd massage you in it." Once dressed, they would meet their wives or girlfriends waiting for them in a windowless room under the stands and then go out for a night on the town.

In 1952, the FA inaugurated a national football competition for youth players between the ages of fifteen and eighteen, which they named The FA Youth Challenge Cup. This was an opportunity for the big clubs of the day to give their youth players a first-hand taste of knock-out football. Busby and Murphy jumped at the chance. The youth policy at United had brought together a group of indisputably brilliant players, but their gifts needed to be tested under conditions other than local leagues and training sessions. The Youth Cup would provide exactly those conditions and Busby and Murphy set about assembling their team for the first year's competition. Albert Scanlon, who was part of that first year's team, recalls how he was selected and how the team progressed:

"I was playing in this B team, Colts they call it, and we were meeting outside the Queen's, as I say, and Bert Fishburn got me, he says, 'Go and get a bus and report to the Cliff'. So I says, 'I don't want to…' He says, 'Go and do as you're told, go and get…' So I walked down Market Street, Victoria bus station, got the thirteen, got off at Cromwell and went to the Cliff and Jack Pauline was in charge of the B team and he says, 'You're playing centre forward for the Colts', which is a big step up for me, because lads the same age as me were playing in the Reserves, but I was only little and then I never went back to the juniors. And then they started sneaking me in the A team and then they got that Youth Cup going and that was a thing that broadened it all out, the first year of Youth Cup. And the last four teams in the Youth Cup was Brentford, Manchester United, Wolves and Huntley and Palmer's Biscuit Works. And Wolves drew Huntley and Palmer's, we drew Brentford. The week before there was a fellow in the paper, Cliff Evans, that wrote about junior football, and he said the best team he'd ever seen was Brentford and they'd walk away with this youth cup and we drew 'em in the semi-final. And we went on a Friday, and Jimmy give a team talk before the game and you line up and there's always a table in and he's got the ball, they only ever give you one ball, and he'd say, 'Right lads' and he'd say to Bert, 'Have we got any Cockneys in here?' And Bert'd go, 'Gordon and Duncan are from Cannock, Bryce is Scotch, Billy's from southern Ireland, Eddie's Salford, Albert and Eddie Lewis are from Manchester, Duncan, Dudley, Ronnie Cope, Crewe, Dave is from Yorkshire, no we've not got any' he'd say, and he threw the ball at Ronnie. He said, 'Well go out' and he says, 'I hate these southern bastards' he says, 'you've got to beat these today'. And that's how he'd get you, and we beat 'em two one, and we beat 'em six down here."

Playing alongside Albert Scanlon in that team were Eddie Colman, Duncan Edwards, David Pegg and Billy Whelan. Ninety-three clubs entered the competition in its first year, including Wolverhampton Wanderers, Manchester United's biggest rivals. Wolves managed to see off Huntley and Palmer's Biscuit Works in the semis and met United for the Final. The first leg was played at Old Trafford in May 1953, with United winning 7-1. The return leg at Molineux ended a 2-2 draw, so United won 9-3 on aggregate. It was a magnificent achievement for Busby and his young team.

The second year of the competition saw the number of entrants grow. Hoping to win the Cup this time round were wonderfully-named clubs such as White Rose of York, Battle Athletic of Reading and Longfleet St Mary's of Dorset. But these teams were no match for the bigger clubs and the Final was a repeat of the previous year's. The first leg, at Wolves, ended in a 4-4 draw, with Edwards and Pegg scoring two apiece, while an astonishing 28,000 people attended the return leg at Old Trafford to watch David Pegg score from the penalty spot in a narrow 1-0 final score. United had done it again.

United cruised to their third final in 1955, meeting West Bromwich Albion. Along the way, they were drawn against, and beat, some huge clubs: Liverpool, Manchester City, Sheffield Wednesday and Chelsea. In the first leg of the final at Old Trafford, Eddie Colman was captain and the hero of the hour, scoring twice in a 4-1 win. In the away leg at The Hawthorns, United won 3-0 and coasted to a 7-1 win on aggregate.

The FA had introduced a three-year eligibility rule into the competition, which meant that no player could play more than three years in succession. Whilst it provided continuity, it also meant that, in the fourth year of the competition, United had to drop Duncan Edwards and Eddie Colman from the side – in their place came the newly-signed youngster from Swansea, Kenny Morgans. United beat Preston North End, Sunderland and Bolton Wanderers, among others, to reach the Final against Chesterfield. Playing for Chesterfied that day was a young goalkeeper called Gordon Banks. Despite Banks' obvious quality, Bobby Charlton managed to put one past him in a 3-2 win at Old Trafford. In the return leg, a 1-1 draw was enough for United to retain the Cup.

The three-year rule meant that United lost Bobby Charlton for the 1956-57 campaign, but the youth team still powered their way to the Final once again, beating Burnley, Huddersfield Town and Blackburn Rovers on the way. The first leg of the Final against West Ham United at Upton Park was a 3-2 win for United. The Old Trafford return match saw United trounce West Ham 5-0. United had won the Cup for an incredible fifth year in a row. The names of United's team for the Final in 1957, with one exception, makes for unfamiliar reading: Gaskell, Smith, Maddison, English, Holland, Bratt, Morgans, Lawton, Dawson, Pearson, Hunter. The more familiar 'Babes' had all moved into the first team, but it is a testament to the depth and breadth of the club as a whole that these relatively unknown players were able to win the Cup as well.

For many reasons, the Youth Cup was an important stepping stone for all the young United players taking part. Firstly, they were playing boys of their own age, which was often not the case when they played for the junior A and B teams in the local and county leagues. The skills they had picked up playing against dockers and factory workers, who continually hacked them down, shone through against less physical opposition. It was a chance to show off their natural ability. Secondly, they gained invaluable experience playing at the big grounds belonging to the First Division sides, grounds like Stamford Bridge, Anfield, Maine Road and Deepdale, where the crowds were as large as 20,000. This was a far cry from the farms, chopped-up fields and park pitches on which they were used to playing.

It also set off in their young minds the winning mentality. Until they could secure a first team place, winning the Youth Cup was the greatest achievement for any youth side. The FA's three-year eligibility rule gave them the opportunity to play in consecutive competitions and this allowed them to build on their success. Furthermore, not only could players taste the glory of winning the Cup once, but they had to return as Champions and learn to defend their trophy, which is arguably more difficult than winning it in the first place.

From the club's perspective, winning the Youth Cup five times in a row was testament to the magnificent job done by Joe Armstrong and the whole scouting team. It was obvious to everyone that the Youth Policy was working superlatively well – so talented and young was the squad of 'Babes' that Busby didn't need to buy a single player between 1953 and 1957. During this incredible five-year winning streak, no fewer than 20 teenagers made their debuts for Manchester United.

The competition had generated large amounts of money for the club and its young team were garnering the kind of media interest that was the envy of many. This, of course, augured well for Busby's young side as it taught them how to deal with being in the public domain and the media spotlight. Most of all, however, it showed the club that Busby had been right to make the demands that he had when he joined the club. He had asked them to place their total trust in him and give him absolute power and now he was showing them what he could do with such things at his disposal.

Following their third consecutive win in 1955, the FA presented United with plaque to commemorate their achievement. To go on and win five in a row was unbelievable, and ranks as one of Busby's greatest achievements as Manager. Between 1952 and 1957, United played 46 games in the Youth Cup, winning 39 of them, drawing six and losing just once, against Southampton in the second leg of the semi-final in 1957. More than fifty years later, there isn't a single club that has come anywhere near to emulating in that competition what United did during the fifties.

It was around this time that the team became referred to regularly as the 'Busby Babes'. The term had been first coined by the *Manchester Evening News* in November 1951 in a write up of United's goalless draw at Anfield because the game marked the debuts of Roger Byrne and Jackie Blanchflower. Busby always hated the term for its connotations of naivety

– he much preferred 'Red Devils' – but, for many, the name summed up the charm and grace of this squad of players and their relationship with their figurehead. Manchester United was now the most talked-about team in the country. Everyone wanted to know who was playing in the first team and how it did. As well as winning the Youth Cup, they also won the League Championship in '56 and '57. The players became as famous as film stars – indeed, when Harry Gregg joined the side in November 1957, he described Manchester United as "the Hollywood of football". They were at the top of their game, without peer. It seemed as though there was absolutely nothing this exciting, fabulously-talented, audacious side couldn't achieve.

3

THE PLAYERS

Among the players who came through the Youth Policy to the first team were: Geoffrey Bent; Roger Byrne; Jackie Blanchflower; Bobby Charlton; Eddie Colman; Duncan Edwards; Bill Foulkes; Mark Jones; Kenny Morgans; Dave Pegg; Albert Scanlon; Dennis Viollet and Liam Whelan. Strictly speaking, Johnny Berry, Harry Gregg, Tommy Taylor and Ray Wood were not Busby Babes because they were bought from other clubs rather than being brought up locally or brought up through Manchester United's Youth Policy system. But this is the only difference between them. Although he was bought as a professional, for instance, Tommy Taylor shared a room with Jackie Blanchflower at Mrs Watson's boarding house and spent all his time with the other players and so, in every sense of the word, they were as much a part of the team as anyone. With an average age of just 21, the first XI that won the League Division One Championship in 1955/56 was one of, if not *the* youngest, ever to win it.

Geoffrey Bent is the least well known of the United players who travelled to Belgrade. A natural left-back, it was sheer bad timing that he happened to be at the club at the same time as Roger Byrne, to whom he remained an understudy throughout his entire professional career. He never established a first-team place and, in his ten years at the club, he was only in the starting line-up as cover for Byrne on twelve occasions. Two leg-breaks during his career didn't help matters. Despite not being able to shift Byrne from his spot, however, everyone knew his quality as a player. He was easily the best of the United players who could not get into the first team and he would have, without doubt, secured a regular first-team place at any other First Division club. Indeed, round about the time of the crash, Wolves showed strong interest in him and Bent asked Busby for a transfer, but Matt Busby wouldn't let him go, saying that everyone in the squad was a first-team player.

Bent was born on the 27th September 1932 in Salford. His father worked as a washer on the rail trucks at Sandhole Colliery. As a boy, Bent was a very strong swimmer and qualified as a lifeguard. When he was thirteen, Bent was presented with a medal from the 'Humane Society for the Hundred of Salford' for rescuing a boy from drowning in Salford Canal. The following year, he played at Old Trafford on the way to winning the English Schools' Trophy with Salford Boys. Bent was captain. He joined United on leaving school in the summer of 1948 and, after several seasons playing in the youth and reserve sides, he signed as a professional in 1951. While a youth at United, Bent worked as a joiner in the same firm as Duncan Edwards.

He was one of the eight Manchester United players who lost their lives at Munich. He didn't play any first-team games during the 1957-58 season, and so was surprised to be told that he would go to Belgrade – Roger Byrne had picked up an injury to his thigh and it wasn't certain that he would be able to play. Bent didn't want to go. He hated flying – it caused him terrible nosebleeds and he had to use drops for the pain in his ears. Besides, Bent knew Byrne would be fit and he said so to his wife. As it turned out, he was right.

Bent met his wife, Marion, when he started dating Marion's younger sister, Betty. He had split up with Betty when, one night at a dance at the Swinton Palais, Bent saw Marion and asked her for a dance – he was seventeen and she was nineteen. They married in 1953 and, like many other of the players, lived on the King's Road. All the time Bent was at United, he was aware that his livelihood as a professional player was limited, so he carried on with his joinery in the summers. When Marion became pregnant, he made a cot for the baby. His daughter, Karen, was born just four months before his death. When Karen was eleven, she and her mother were invited to Wembley for the 1968 European Cup Final.

Born in Aldershot in June 1926, Johnny 'Digger' Berry was one of the older members of United's first team and, along with Roger Byrne, a survivor from the 1951/52 Championship winning side – but it could all have been so different for Johnny Berry. When he left school, Berry became a trainee cinema projectionist and only discovered he had any footballing talent when he played in the Army while he served in India during the Second World War. In that Army team was a man called Fred Harris, who was the captain of Birmingham City before the War broke out. When the War ended, it was Harris who brought Berry to Birmingham City, for whom he played on the right wing until 1951. It was during his last season at Birmingham City that Berry scored one of the most sensational goals ever seen against Manchester United at Old Trafford. To add insult to injury, Berry's goal won the match for Birmingham. Busby was impressed, so much so that he immediately bought Berry for £25,000.

Both Johnny Berry and Roger Byrne were in the unusual position of having played a major part in two of Busby's three great United teams. They had played with all the big names that had won the FA Cup Final in 1948 and the Championship in 1952, and yet they mingled with the younger players in a way that the older players hadn't when they were young. In that sense, they held a unique position of bridging the gap between the old and the new.

Making his first team debut, Albert Scanlon remembers this mix of the young and not-so-young very well: "I went in [to the first team] at Hibernian, so that was me first game as a kid. There was Wood, Foulkes, Byrne, Don Gibson, Big Allenby, Freddie Goodwin, Johnny Berry, Jackie Blanchflower, Tommy Taylor – I can't remember the inside left, it wasn't Dennis because he was in the forces – and myself. We're in this hotel and we had a meal and I'd gone out and got this paper. I come back and they was all playing cards and a big chap walked in, well dressed, and he got hold of Tom, 'cos everything went through Tom Curry, and he put six bottles of whisky on this little bar and Tom went round and he give everybody a fiver and he says, 'The chairman of Hibernian has given you all five pound because you're the first team that's beat 'em at Easter Road for five years'. And these six bottles of whisky were for Matt and the directors. And all of a sudden, Tom got up and there's no whisky. Gone, completely gone. So he's going on about this and he's saying, 'Well, we've not moved'. And about an hour later the door opened and Johnny Berry fell in and he wanted water and ice. Well Johnny was sort of same age as Allenby, they were the old type, you know, had come after the war, brilliant people. And they'd signed Johnny from Birmingham, 'cos he'd murdered United and they paid a lot of money at Birmingham for him. And anyway Tom says, 'Have you got our whisky?' and John said, 'No, no, I've not got your whisky'. And he went to door and Big Allenby was huge, oh he was, he was huge and I always remember, he used to have his hair parted down the middle and he always wore a scarf, grey or yellow scarf, he was a big hunk of a fellow. And he was there, so Tom knew where the whisky had gone but he didn't chase it with Allenby, 'cos Allenby was captain you see. And nobody ever told the boss that this whisky had been left for him 'cos Allenby and John had drank it."

Standing just 5'7" tall, Berry was one of the smallest players at United, but he was also one of the fastest. His pace and clever, direct play ensured that he could get to the by-line and cross into the box nearly every time. But he also had one eye constantly on the goal, scoring 45 goals in 276 appearances for United. Although he cost a considerable amount of money, Berry was one of Busby's shrewder and more successful buys. He collected three championship medals with United and four England caps.

Berry was one of the worst injured at Munich. In the Munich hospital, he was put in an upstairs room for the critically injured, along with Duncan Edwards, Jackie Blanchflower and Matt Busby. Initially, he was given less chance of survival than Duncan Edwards but, against the odds, he did survive. He never fully recovered physically or mentally after Munich, though, and shortly afterwards he was given his employment cards and told to give up his club house. A year after Munich, he returned to his hometown of Aldershot where he opened a sports shop with his brother and remained for the rest of his life. He died in 1994.

Jackie Blanchflower, known as 'Blanchy' to his team mates (ironically, since he had jet-black hair) was born and brought up in Protestant East Belfast. His older, more famous brother Danny played for Tottenham Hotspur. Both brothers were taught football by their mother, who played for a ladies' team in Belfast. Their father was an iron-turner in the shipyards. Like his brother, Blanchflower was quietly spoken and highly intelligent. He was spotted by United's scouts in Northern Ireland and signed for United in March 1949, aged 15. He was one of the very first Busby Babes to arrive at United.

On the day Blanchflower arrived in Manchester, he was
met at Victoria train station by Busby and taken to Busby's
house for breakfast. After breakfast, he was taken to Old
Trafford, which was still being refurbished. The place was
deserted, the pitch full of weeds. For Blanchflower, it was all
in stark contrast to the glamour of United's famous victory at
Wembley in 1948. He went to his digs at Mrs Browne's and
reported for work as a plumber the next day.

Initially, he started playing as an inside-forward but, as new
players came to the club, he couldn't keep out the likes of
Dennis Viollet and Bill Whelan from that position and so, like
many other players before him, Busby tried him further down
the pitch. If he couldn't keep his place as an inside-forward,
he certainly wasn't going to keep out the likes of Duncan
Edwards or Eddie Colman at wing-half. Then, fortuitously,
he was picked to play for Northern Ireland at centre-half,
where he flourished. It was now obvious to everyone where
his natural position was and he started to play for the Reserves
at centre-half.

Even in this position, however, there was very stiff
competition from Mark Jones and the two players were always
vying for the centre-half role. Off the pitch, however, they
were the best of friends and ended up sharing a room at
Mrs Watson's. Bill Foulkes and Roger Byrne were already
established in the junior A team, at right-back and left-back
respectively, and these four players would form the basis of the
United defence for most of the next nine years. Playing open-
age football in the local leagues, the A team won everything,
including the top junior trophy, the Gylcriss Cup.

Blanchflower was a very stylish and constructive defender,
which went against the grain of most centre halves of the day.
He might have lacked pace, but he was highly skillful and could
read the game expertly. Instead of making lunging tackles and
bringing players down, he robbed them of the ball by making

clever interceptions or by clearing the ball from their feet. His fantastic abilities at both passing and heading the ball made him the complete centre-half. Blanchflower made his debut in the First XI against Liverpool at Anfield in November 1951, the same day as Roger Byrne, but it would take another season before he established his place in the first team.

When Tommy Taylor was signed by United in March 1953, he moved into Mrs Watson's house and he and Blanchflower struck up an immediate friendship and became as close as brothers. On one of United's trips to the Norbreck Hydro hotel in Blackpool, where the team always spent a few days relaxing together before a big game, he and Tommy Taylor once walked up to the hotel bar naked except for their United ties and ordered a drink. Blanchflower and Taylor had a party piece where they used to have a mock fight and they performed it in public whenever they could. They had it down so well that onlookers really did think they were punching the living daylights out of each other. They shared a common love of boxing and Taylor became Blanchflower's 'trainer'. Blanchflower even went as far as entering a few bouts, sending any fees he received back home to his mother. It was never much, though, as Blanchflower nearly always lost.

In May 1957, Blanchflower married a singer, Jean, who was extremely attractive. Here's Albert Scanlon on how Blanchflower met Jean: "...there was a show on at the Opera House and in this show, whichever it was, was Shani Wallis who was a big star and she was in *Oliver* with Alec Guinness and Robert Newton, but she was on the stage now. And she fell head over heels [for Jackie], she'd have given Blanchflower anything he wanted, she adored Jackie Blanchflower. Jackie went with Tommy to a British Legion a few months later, and there was a girl on called Jean, a singer, Jackie saw her and that was it. She was as rough as a dog's arse, she drank, she swore and Jackie saw Jean and that was it. Shani Wallis might as well

have been on the planet Mars. And he got married and people
tried to talk him out of it. She was rough and ready, Jean, but
she was good company, oh she was brilliant."

Blanchflower was amongst the worst injured in the Munich
aircrash. When he came to, Blanchflower found himself lying
in the snow, pinned down by the body of Roger Byrne. Very
close to his face, on Byrne's wrist, was Byrne's watch, the
second hand still ticking. Byrne didn't have a mark on his
body, but his back was broken and he had died immediately
in the crash. Blanchflower remembered that watch for the
rest of his life. Like Johnny Berry, Blanchflower never fully
recovered from his injuries and he never played football again.

Life after Manchester United was difficult for Blanchflower,
and his family lived in straitened circumstances. He tried
his hand at various jobs – buying and running a sweet shop,
working with a bookie, working as a finance officer, as a
landlord, none of which worked out. In his later years he
became a successful after-dinner speaker. "He used to go with
Jean to these Legions and clubs," Scanlon remembers, "and
one day she says, 'You can earn money'. He says, 'How can I
earn money?' And she sat him down in front of the bedroom
mirror and wrote little pieces for him, jokes and all that and
did his timing, got his timing right and he became an after
dinner speaker in his own right, he was one of the best, he
was." After losing his battle against cancer, Jackie Blanchflower
died in 1998.

Roger Byrne, the Captain, was the linchpin in Busby's team.
When he first joined the club, he was a hot-headed 20-year
old who had a problem with authority, but he later became
much calmer and was very well respected by management
and, being slightly older, players alike. According to Harry
Gregg, Byrne could give off the impression of being "aloof

and big-headed", but he says that Byrne was actually much quieter and more thoughtful than most people realised. Jackie Blanchflower said he could be "cantankerous" at times, but Byrne was clearly the kind of man who didn't care what people thought of him. He wasn't at all concerned about his image, or the image of the team – all that mattered was his drive and ambition to win.

Being included in the pre-match talks between Busby and Murphy, he was the player on the pitch who carried out Busby's instructions. He was an enforcer, a player who wasn't afraid to let a team mate know, in no uncertain terms, if he was performing under par or not giving his all. He led by example, and expected everyone else to do so. But, under Busby, Byrne learnt perhaps an even more important lesson – how to take criticism. His youthful rashness developed into mature self-examination. What he was never able to do, however, was take criticism of the team from anyone outside of it. "You can criticise me," he said, "but don't criticise my team."

Born in September 1929, Byrne grew up in Gorton, Manchester. His father worked in the furniture department at Lewis's department store. Byrne earned a scholarship to Burnage Grammar School where he played on the left wing for the school team and then went on to play for Burnage Boys. He did his National Service with the Air Force, for whom he also played football. When he returned to Manchester, he continued playing for various amateur teams, but the thought of becoming a professional footballer had never really crossed his mind – he just loved the physical exercise and competitive spirit. Through their scouting system, United eventually heard about a promising local winger who played for Ryder Brow Boys and the club gave Byrne a trail in 1949. He was taken on.

He developed under the generation of great players (Jack Rowley, Stan Pearson, Johnny Carey, *et al*) who had won the FA Cup in 1948 and made his debut in November 1951, the same day as Jackie Blanchflower. When he first joined at Manchester United, he played on the left wing but, as was the case with many new players, it took a while for Busby and Murphy to work out where best to use him. He was eventually moved to left-back, which is where he flourished. Once they had found his natural position, Byrne made an immediate impact on the team, securing a regular first-team place much more quickly than any of the other newcomers. One of the fastest players in the side, he could sprint up the wing, but was always fast enough to get back in time. Byrne wasn't a tackler like most left-backs of the day because no one could pass him. He timing was perfect, he didn't need to lunge. Busby described him as an "aristocratic footballer, majestic in his movement."

During these early years, though, Byrne was still very impetuous and Busby had to reprimand him for ill-discipline many times and reigning in his reckless tendencies was a real headache for Busby. After winning the Championship in 1952, Manchester United embarked on an eight-week tour of North America. Byrne went, along with Jackie Blanchflower, Mark Jones and Dennis Viollet. They sailed on the *Queen Elizabeth* and played at the New York Yankee Stadium, as well as playing matches in Chicago, Detroit, Toronto, Montreal and Vancouver. In Los Angeles, Manchester United were due to play Atlas, the champions of Mexico and a team with a terrible reputation for playing dirty. Before the match, Busby warned his players of this and ordered them not to retaliate. "Just ignore it," Busby said, "walk away." Of course, Byrne lost his temper on the pitch and got himself sent off. Busby was furious. He told Byrne to pack his bags because he was sending him home. Byrne was distraught, in tears at the thought of returning home under such a cloud of shame. That evening, Carey spoke to Busby, telling him how remorseful Byrne was. Busby told Carey that Byrne would have to stand up and make a full apology to the rest of the team. The following morning, Byrne did so and the matter was dropped.

This was the turning point for Byrne. When the team returned to England, Carey retired and Busby chose to make Byrne the Captain. Busby was taking a huge risk but, once again, his decision turned out to be a masterstroke. From then on, Byrne became a different man altogether. The trust Busby placed in him allowed him to grow authoritatively into his role as Captain and Byrne ended up making a huge return on Busby's initial risk. In all, Byrne played 246 league games for club and 33 internationals for country. By the time of his death, Roger Byrne was England's first choice left-back, one of those players whose inclusion in the team is so taken for granted that it wasn't even discussed.

Byrne was an incredibly physical player, a fitness fanatic who used the gym more than any other player. He would often go coatless in winter because he thought the cold kept him sharp. Realising that a footballing career was a short one, he began training at Salford Royal Hospital to become a physiotherapist. When he was there, he didn't want his job to set him apart from the other students on his course, so he kept quiet about what he did for a living. It was during his afternoons studying at the hospital that he met his wife-to-be, Joy, who always thought of him as a physiotherapist first and a footballer second. They were married in June 1957. They honeymooned in Jersey and returned to find that their house had been decked out in red and white streamers by his team mates. He also wrote a newspaper column for the *Manchester Evening News* while playing in the first team. Like Jackie Blanchflower, he was a keen golfer – an unusual sport in those days – and he once got a hole-in-one at St Andrew's.

After United controversially lost to Aston Villa in the 1957 FA Cup final, he promised the fans that United would return to Wembley the following year. It is typical of Byrne that he was true to his word, but he never made it to the final. He was killed instantly at Munich and United went on to lose at Wembley, to Bolton Wanderers. At the time of his death, unbeknownst to Byrne, his wife was four months pregnant. His son was named Roger Byrne Junior. He was a ball-boy at Old Trafford for three years.

Bobby Charlton is one of the giants of modern football. Apart from one season at Preston North End at the end of his career, Charlton played all his football at Manchester United, making a record 751 appearances and scoring 245 goals. No one has come anywhere close to scoring as many goals for United, and his record as England's top goalscorer remains intact.

Born in October 1937 in the mining town of Ashington in Northumberland, he comes from a famous footballing family. One of his uncles was the great Jackie Milburn, the Newcastle and England striker, and his brother is Jackie Charlton. His other uncles George, Jack and Jim all played for Leeds United, while another uncle, Stan, played for Leicester City. Despite all the footballers in his family, however, it was his mother, Cissie, who was the first to coach both her sons. Later, as a young lad, he remembers going to football matches at St James' with his uncles, who would pass him overhead to the front of the crowd. His favourite player was Stanley Mathews. Charlton's uncles pointed out to the young lad that what marked Matthews out from the rest was his speed over the first ten yards. Charlton never forgot that comment and his grandfather, who was a professional trainer of sprinters, used to teach him how to run.

Charlton was spotted and immediately signed by Joe Armstrong when he was just fifteen and not yet out of school. Arriving at Old Trafford, he shared a room at Mrs Watson's with David Pegg, who showed Charlton around and took him out with the others in the evenings. Shy and unprepossessing, Charlton idolised the confident and charming Pegg, recognising in Pegg the qualities he himself lacked. According to Harry Gregg, Charlton was "surly" and difficult to get to know, but he was particularly liked by Jimmy Murphy.

When he first signed to the club, he was one of the youngest of the Babes and, during the 1955/56 season, found it impossible to get into the first team because all the players in it were playing so well. The team won the Championship at the end of that season. Frustratingly for Charlton, they started playing even better the following season. Charlton was becoming desperate. He continued to play for the reserves, regularly scoring two or three goals in scorelines like 9-0, but then, to make matters worse, he twisted his right ankle and was out for a few weeks. At the end of September 1956, both Edwards and Taylor were injured in a match against Arsenal and were ruled out for the next couple of games. "How's your ankle?" Busby asked Charlton. "Fine," he said, although in reality it was far from all right. It wasn't sore when he ran, but when he turned on it or tried to kick the ball, it hurt like hell, but Charlton knew he wouldn't get another chance and so he lied. Busby selected him for the following week's game and Charlton made his debut, aged 18, against Charlton Athletic, ironically enough, scoring two goals. "I never kicked the ball with my right foot all day," Charlton said.

It's easy to forget how young Charlton actually was – just 20 – when the Munich Air Crash happened. He was thrown clear, still strapped into his seat, and suffered only minor injuries to the head. He was in hospital for no longer than a week. Charlton was lucky enough to be one of the few players who survived Munich both physically and professionally and, along with Bill Foulkes, he went on to be part of the side that won the European Cup in 1968. Psychologically, however, Charlton never fully recovered from the tragedy, speaking often of the guilt he has always felt about surviving the crash.

He retired from Manchester United in the early 1970s but joined the board in 1984, where he remains today.

At only 5'5", Eddie Colman was the smallest player in the team. Because of his size, he was often singled out and picked on during games, but Bill Foulkes used to look after him. Not only was Colman small, he looked much younger than his, very few, years as well. Once, just before a game in Blackpool, Colman met his cousin outside the ground in order to give him a ticket for the game. After chatting for a few minutes, Colman tried to get back into the ground but the man on the gate, not believing who Colman said he was, wouldn't let him in and told him to go to the kids' entrance. Colman had to get Matt Busby to come to his rescue before he was allowed back in. As if that wasn't bad enough, the same thing happened again when United played West Bromwich Albion.

According to Harry Gregg, Eddie Colman was "a complete and total, tubby little bugger with puffed out cheeks and a fat arse, a brilliant player." His nickname was 'Snakehips', because of the body swerve he used to shimmy past people during a game. Joe Armstrong once said of him: "Put a grass skirt on him and you've got a hula-hula dancer". He used to push the ball into space and then run and was an absolute expert at dribbling, linking up well on pitch with Duncan Edwards. He was the only member of the squad not in complete awe of Edwards and would often nutmeg him in training just to tease him. He was very fast, even faster than Roger Byrne, but the fastest in the team over 100 yards was Ray Wood.

Born in November 1936 in Archie Street (the model for 'Coronation Street') in Salford, Colman was the only child of Dick and Elizabeth. His father was unemployed for five years during the Depression. Dick Colman was a talented footballer in his own right and used to play for Ordsall Centre, a team made up exclusively of unemployed men. They won the Salford Unemployed Cup Final in 1933, a game played at Old Trafford. As a winner's prize, each man was given a new pair of boots. Dick Colman, however, scored a hat-trick in the game and, in addition to his boots, was given a brand new suit, which he pawned for £1.

Colman grew up playing football on the bombed-out sites of Manchester. Very streetwise from an early age, he was, apparently, bit of a local villain until he was 15, a loveable rogue thereafter. He was one of the most popular players, always at the centre of any celebrations or sing-a-longs. He was also an incorrigible practical joker. At United, he was closest to David Pegg and Tommy Taylor, who were also great practical jokers. The three of them were known as the Old Trafford Crazy Gang. At the Norbreck Hydro Hotel, where the players often stayed, each room had an alarm with its own unique tone. One gag of Colman's was to synchronise all these alarms (apart from his own, of course) to go off simultaneously at some ungodly hour.

One of the original Babes, he joined the club when he left school in the summer of 1952, playing his way up through the junior and reserve teams until his first-team debut aged 19, in November 1955 against Bolton Wanderers. During his time at the club, he did two years National Service in the Royal Corps of Signals at Catterick, where he was a physical training instructor and the camp's official 'rat catcher', but he managed to continue playing for United at the weekends. He made 107 first-team appearances, playing at left-half, but in all those games he only scored two goals, the second of which was at Old Trafford in the first leg against Red Star Belgrade. Not a bad time to score.

As a junior player, he was always five minutes late, and would always arrive for training well-dressed. Very clothes conscious, Colman was constantly on the look out for the latest fashion. At first, it was a cloth cap and a striped college scarf. Later, he would try to emulate Frank Sinatra by wearing a pork pie hat.

This would be replaced by the teddy boy look, complete with sideburns and a quiff, drainpipe trousers and winklepicker shoes, which he wore long before anyone else even knew what they were. He loved 30s and 40s jazz – Sidney Bechet and Sarah Vaughan. He also loved flying, preferred it to travelling by car. At the time of the crash, he was planning to marry a young woman named Marjorie, who was a hair model. Marjorie went on to marry another United player, Bobby English. Aged 21 years and three months at the time of the crash, he was the youngest person to die in the Munich Air Disaster.

Eddie Colman had a cousin, Albert Valentine, to whom he was especially close. They lived one street away from each other and grew up playing football together. When Albert heard about his cousin's death, he was immediately plunged into shock and didn't remember anything until the moment he realised he was standing in Piccadilly, Manchester, at three o'clock in the morning, coatless and soaked to the skin. He couldn't eat anything or sleep at all for the following few weeks and slept badly for two more years. Late one night, Albert was lying in bed, unable to sleep as usual, when he heard the sound of a car stop outside his house. He then heard laughter and the car doors being slammed shut followed by the sound of the front door of his house being opened. Then there were footsteps on the stairs. Albert thought they were burglars, so he grabbed a cricket bat and stood waiting behind the door. The bedroom door opened and in walked Eddie and David Pegg. "We're going to the Spare Wheel, are you coming?" they said. Albert said "No" and they left. He heard the front door being closed, then the sound of a car leaving. Albert got back into bed and fell asleep immediately. He never had any problems sleeping after that night.

Duncan Edwards was a colossus of the game, among only a handful of players who truly are the greatest this country has ever produced. According to Matt Busby, Edwards was "the player who had everything". When Edwards was signed by United, Jimmy Murphy said: "he has a great right foot and a great left foot, he is strong in the tackle, he is great in the air, he reads the game and he can play in any position, and he is fast and has tremendous enthusiasm. And when I knock all the rough edges off him, I am going to make him a decent player."

Born on 1st October 1936 in Dudley in the West Midlands, his father, Gladstone, was a metal-polisher and played football at amateur level. Edwards was a huge baby and, according to his mother, could kick a ball before he could walk. One of the first things his mother bought him as a boy was a small football and a pair of boots. She said: "I never had to teach my boy to play football the way Bobby Charlton's mother did. He was just born with the ability. He kicked a ball without anyone ever showing him how."

He attended Wolverhampton Street School and grew up playing football in streets and parks. By the time he was ten years old, Edwards was as big and strong as the sixteen-year-old boys he played against, but he was quiet and very shy off the field. With his school, he reached the final of the Dudley Schools' Under-Fourteen Cup, losing 2-0 to Dudley Grammar. When he was asked by one of his friends what he was going to do after leaving school, he said "I'm going to play for Manchester United." Even though he grew up surrounded by some of the greatest teams of the day, teams like Wolverhampton Wanderers, West Bromwich Albion and Aston Villa, Edwards supported Manchester United and always dreamt of playing for them.

He rose quickly through local and county teams until, in 1950, he was selected for the England Schoolboys team and made Captain. His performances on the field were now earning him a lot of interest from many of the big clubs. Wolves, in particular, badly wanted the local lad. Busby dispatched Joe Armstrong to watch Edwards play. Ten minutes was all Armstrong needed – he told Busby that Busby should approach Edwards' family immediately. When Busby visited Edwards' family in Dudley, they were impressed with his manner. Edwards' mother said, "The first time we met Matt Busby it was obvious that he was a gentleman." Busby instructed Murphy to keep an eye on Edwards, which he did, for two years. Edwards was signed on 1st October 1952 – his sixteenth birthday.

He lodged at Mrs Watson's with the other juniors and started his apprenticeship as a carpenter, but he hated it, so he was put 'on the brush' instead – on the ground staff, painting the stands. He was renowned for his keenness to train and for his physical stamina and would turn up for training in just a polo-neck sweater and a pair of shorts, even on the coldest mornings. He warmed up alone, running laps around the pitch flat out. Physically, the other players simply couldn't keep up with him. During training, he quickly formed a strong partnership with Eddie Colman, the other wing-half in the middle of the pitch. "We used to look at players in training," Matt Busby said, "to see if we might have to get them to concentrate more on their kicking, or their heading or ball control. We looked at Duncan, right at the start, and gave up trying to spot flaws in his game."

He played his first game for Manchester United against Cardiff City on 4th April 1953, when he was still six months shy of his seventeenth birthday. He reputedly did not suffer from nerves before a game. When he first played against Jackie Milburn, the great Newcastle and England centre forward, Edwards walked up to Milburn and said, "Reputations mean nothing to me and if you come near me I'll kick you over the stand." Milburn was livid. For someone so quiet and unassuming off the field, Edwards' huge on-field presence was a remarkable transformation. He was so powerfully built that his team mates used to call him 'Tank'. After the game he walked over to Milburn: "Thanks for the game, Chief," he said. He called everyone "chief". In all, he made 175 appearances in a United shirt, scoring 21 goals. On 2nd April 1955, aged just eighteen years and 183 days, he won the first of his eighteen caps for England. In 1956, he played against West Germany, then the World Cup holders, in Berlin and scored a goal with one of his famous runs, simply brushing the German players aside – a goal that earned him the nickname 'Boom Boom' from the German press. England won 3-1. His ferocious style of play made some spectators call him a dirty player but, although he was a hard tackler, he was fair. Crowds and criticisms left him unmoved, however, and, by the time of his death at twenty-one, he was considered one of the most complete footballers of his generation.

Duncan Edwards was Jimmy Murphy's favourite player in the squad, "the most complete player I have ever seen." Ken Morgans recalls a team talk given by Murphy as Welsh manager: "Wales were playing England and Jimmy went through the Welsh team the same as he went through our team when he talked to us, he would say, watch him do this. Or he would say, this fellow's one-footed, push him across the pitch, don't let him outside with his good foot. And he went through the whole team and he finished the team talk and Reg Davies said, 'Jimmy, you haven't mentioned Duncan Edwards. What do I do?' Jimmy looks up and he said, 'Son, stay out of his effing way'."

Although highly concentrated on football, he was also very aware a career could be short-lived and had a column in the *Manchester Evening News*, and wrote a book *Tackle Soccer This Way*. He was engaged to Molly Leach at time of Munich. Edwards was very shy around girls. He went with the others to the clubs in Manchester on a Saturday night, but all he would do is hang around, not mixing with the girls at all. He met Molly while with a friend at a skating rink called the Ice

House. As soon as he set eyes on her, he walked straight over and started talking to her. A bit taken aback by his directness, Molly wasn't too keen at first, but she gradually fell for him and they were soon inseparable.

He suffered absolutely appalling internal injuries in the air crash. Unaware of the true extent of these, his initial chances of survival seemed better than most of those who were very badly injured, but he died on 21st February, fifteen days after the crash. For many, it was the lowest point of the Munich Air Disaster. When he was just ten-years-old, Edwards' sister, Carole Anne, was born, but she died of meningitis at fourteen weeks old. In 1964, Edwards' father became a Garden Assistant at Queen's Cross Cemetery, where he was able to tend his son's, and his daughter's, grave.

Bill Foulkes was the hard man of the side, the fixer. If Jimmy Murphy wanted an ugly job doing on the pitch, he went to Foulkes. Described by Albert Scanlon and Harry Gregg respectively as "taciturn and difficult" and "a bit of a bully", his team mates called him 'Cowboy' or 'PB', meaning 'Popular Bill', a sarcastic reference to how unpopular he actually was. He rarely ever mixed with the others off the field and, when he did, he hardly ever said a word. Once, when Albert Scanlon came in very late one night, the usually taciturn Foulkes asked, "Where the hell have you been?" to which Scanlon replied, "I've been out feeding your horse." But, like Roger Byrne, Foulkes wasn't in the game in order to win friends or look good. In that sense, the two were alike – indeed, when Byrne died at Munich, it was Foulkes who was appointed as the new captain.

In footballing terms, Foulkes was an 'old school' kind of defender. Busby described him as "a no-nonsense right-back." In training, Murphy used to say to him: "There's the stand, Bill, kick it in there, don't try and pull it down and do anything fancy." He was solid, dependable, yet undistinguished.

Later on in his career, he moved to centre-half, a position he much preferred.

Bill Foulkes was born in January 1932 in St. Helens, Lancashire, and worked there as a miner when he left school. Foulkes was discovered through Manchester United's tried and tested scouting system in 1950 while he was playing for Whiston Boys and joined the club in March of that year. Instead of taking up a new trade, Foulkes carried on working down the St Helens pits while an amateur at the club, catching the train from there to the Cliff on Tuesday and Thursday evenings. After coming through the junior ranks of the club, he turned professional in August 1951 and made his first-team debut against Liverpool in December 1952, a month short of his twenty-first birthday. United won the match 2–1.

He was married to Teresa, a model who was very popular with the other players and their wives and girlfriends. They were an odd couple, seemingly mismatched, but their marriage was a long and successful one. Emerging physically unscathed from the site of the air crash, he was one of the few players to continue to have a successful career with Manchester United after Munich, making a total of 679 appearances for the club. Only Bobby Charlton and Ryan Giggs have played more games for United. He played right-back for England just once, against Northern Ireland in October 1954. His fellow team mates Roger Byrne and Ray Wood played at left-back and in goal that day, too. England won 2-0.

Harry Gregg, United's first choice goalkeeper, is, according to his friend Albert Scanlon, "crackers, daft as a brush", which confirms the myth that all goalkeepers are mad. Red-haired and fiery, 'Greggy' was the tallest and heaviest member of the team. He was born on 27th October 1932 in Tobermore, County Derry, into a large Protestant family who moved to Coleraine soon after. He always wanted to play football and used to pray each night to get his caps.

"In those days," Gregg says, "I would go across to the Coleraine ground – you wouldn't pay to go in, boys don't pay, you climbed the fence – and Coleraine Reserves were playing the second, third biggest club in Ireland at the time – Linfield, their reserve team, and as I climbed over the corrugated iron and dropped down, the groundsman grabbed me and he marched me, I mean by the ear, across to the dressing rooms and I thought I was in serious trouble and a fellow called Jim White who was in charge of the reserve team said to me, 'Have you any boots?' and I said, 'No, why?'. He said, 'We're short of a goalkeeper'. So I said, 'I can borrow a pair' and I ran a hundred and fifty yards to our street and I borrowed a pair of boots which were a size too small for me, but I wanted to play. And I went back to the Showgrounds and I played against Linfield Swifts and the score was four nil and they gave me fifteen shillings and never spoke to me again."

Ironically, however, it was for Linfield Swifts that Gregg started his career, taken on as a goalkeeper when he left school. "I hated keeping goals," Gregg says, "I played left back and only had a right foot, which was crazy and they said I was too rough, so they put me in goals, which I hated." After three years with Linfield, he moved to Coleraine, still in goal, and it was from there that he was signed by Peter Doherty, manager of Doncaster Rovers, in October 1952. He was nineteen when he made the move across the Irish Sea.

After a string of bad results and indifferent form by Ray Wood, Busby acted quickly and ruthlessly, signing Gregg from Doncaster on the last day of November 1957. By now, Gregg was twenty-five and one of the best keepers in the country. Busby consulted Blanchflower before signing Gregg as he knew that Gregg and Blanchflower had been friends since boyhood and had both played for Irish Schoolboys. Blanchflower, and his wife Jean, were at Victoria Station to greet him when Gregg arrived in Manchester. Also there were

Busby and Murphy, as well as several press photographers –
United had paid £23,000 for Gregg, the highest price paid
for a goalkeeper at that time, and the press were curious to
see this hot-blooded Ulsterman. He made his debut, along
with Kenny Morgans, on 21st December against Leicester,
whom they demolished 4-0.

For his first three months at United, Gregg commuted
between Doncaster and Manchester whilst waiting for a club
house to become available. Whenever he was in Manchester, he
was put up by either Jackie Blanchflower or Roger Byrne. He
eventually moved into a club house on the Sunday morning
before the crash. Gregg remembers those first few months of
life at United as being very different from his old club. Training
at Doncaster went on every day of the week, yet at United
the players had Mondays and Tuesday mornings off. Doncaster
banned all drink in the dressing rooms, but at United there
were crates of beer up stacked against the 'kicking board', the
piece of wood the players kicked to get their boots on. The day
before a big game, United took the team out to Daveyhulme
golf course, where the players relaxed over a few rounds of
golf and a meal before being driven to the ground for kick-
off the following morning. It was all a far cry from Doncaster.

On his style of play, Gregg says, "Some people play the
game one way and some people play it the other. I was a person
couldn't stay in the cage and I remember Ray Wood, who was
a good lad, but Ray kept goals on the goal line and stopped
shots. I by nature would come and give stuff out there and
if you happened to get in my way, whether it was one of my
team or the opposition it didn't matter." He was one of the first
goalkeepers to come off his line regularly, and he barged and
punched anything in his way. Albert Scanlon, who was in the
Leicester game as well, remembers: "We was playing Leicester
and they all thought Harry smoked during the game, but he
had smelling salts – and they used to think he smoked on the

pitch. I think we was either winning or drawing at halftime and he was satisfied, the gaffer, so he just wanders round and he tells you little bits and Roger [Byrne, the captain] says, 'Can I ask you to do something for us boss?' and he says, 'What's that?' He says, 'Harry' he says, 'Yeah' he says, 'Will you tell him we're in red 'cos he's gonna kill somebody'."

Mark Jones was one of United's two outstanding centre-halves that the club had during the 1950s, the other being Jackie Blanchflower. Along with Blanchflower, Jones was one of the original Babes and the two of them were part of the team that came after the older, established players like Byrne and Berry and which paved the way for the next generation of players, like Bobby Charlton and Duncan Edwards. A Yorkshireman through and through, Jones was born on 15th June 1933, in the Low Valley, about four miles from Barnsley. His father was a time-keeper at the local colliery. Big and broad-shouldered, he had blond hair and a round face but, although built like a giant, Jones had an especially gentle nature.

He was captain of England Boys when he was spotted by United scouts and signed in 1948. Jones lodged at Mrs Watson's, where he shared a room with Jackie Blanchflower, and worked in the building trade. When the 'youngsters' arrived at Mrs Watson's, they all looked up to Jones as an elder statesman, despite only being twenty-two himself, because of his first-team experience. But they saw little of him. He had started courting a young girl called June when he was fifteen and went back to Barnsley every weekend to see her. It wasn't until a few months into their courtship that he mentioned he was signed to Manchester United as a footballer – June thought he was just a bricklayer. They were married in 1955 and moved into Jack Crompton's old house on the King's Road. They had a son, Gary, and at the time of the air crash, June was pregnant with their second child, a daughter named Lynn.

Jones was an archetypal 'stopper' in the mould of Allenby Chilton, his boyhood hero. As with Bill Foulkes, who arrived at United the year after Jones, Murphy spent hours drilling the basics of defending into Jones during training sessions. "Nothing fancy, just boot the bloody ball over the stand," Murphy would say. He was very good in the air, the best header of the ball at United, according to many, and made his debut against Sheffield Wednesday in the 1951/52 season when Chilton injured himself. He and Jackie Blanchflower were always jockeying for the centre-half position, although they were the best of friends and Jackie was best man at Jones' wedding.

Despite living in Manchester for years, Jones remained a country boy at heart. He always wore a trilby, tweeds and smoked a pipe. He bred budgies and canaries and was nicknamed 'Dan Archer', a character in the Radio Four series 'The Archers' because of his love of country life. He liked nothing more than walking his dog in the country and shooting. He owned a shotgun, which he used to keep in a cupboard at Old Trafford. Walter Crickmer kept one there, too, and the two of them used the guns to keep the pigeon population in the ground under control. Many new arrivals at United were startled, to say the least, by the sight of Jones and Crickmer, blasting away around the stands, slaughtering the birds.

Not a big drinker, like some in the team. At a birthday party, Eddie Colman once replaced the pineapple juice in Jones' glass with whisky and bet Mark Jones that he couldn't drink the bottle of juice in one go. Not knowing it was whisky, Jones said "Of course I can." The whisky knocked him out and he and his wife had to stay the night.

Accompanied by fellow Yorkshiremen Tommy Taylor and David Pegg, Jones sang *On Ilkley Moor Baht'at* for the guests on the night of the banquet in Belgrade. "Mark Jones was singing at the top of his voice," Harry Gregg recalls. "He was a lovely man." When he returned to the site the day after the crash to look through the wreckage, Harry Gregg found Jones' trilby and brought it back from Munich with him. He visited June and offered it to her, but she insisted that Gregg keep it. June also gave away his 50-odd budgies. She put an ad in the local paper and, the next day, dozens of children appeared at her house, forming a queue all the way down King's Road.

Ken Morgans was born in Swansea, in 1939, and grew up playing football on the beaches near the city when the tide had gone out. As his father had before him, Morgans played for Swansea Schoolboys and Welsh Schoolboys. He was signed by United in the summer of 1955, when he was fifteen, after being spotted by Jimmy Murphy and Matt Busby playing for Welsh Schoolboys in a game at Maine Road. The game was due to be played at Wembley, but the turf at Wembley had been dug up, so the fixture was moved to Manchester. The sixteen-year-old Morgans made the thirteen-hour train journey from Swansea to Manchester on his own and was met at the station by Joe Armstrong.

He had a room at Mrs Evans', a boarding house three doors away from where Duncan Edwards lived and five doors down from Tommy Taylor but, although he saw both players in the street all the time, he didn't dare speak to them. They would have told him where to go if he had tried. A natural right winger, Morgans worked his way up through the junior B and A teams, Colts, Reserves for three years, finally getting his chance in the first team when he was eighteen after Johnny Berry had had a bad spell. He made his debut, along with Harry Gregg, against Leicester City and the two of them were first-team choices from then on.

Morgans linked up particularly well with Tommy Taylor on the pitch. Morgans and Taylor used to train together, the diminutive Morgans watching in awe as Taylor did thirty laps around the pitch to start off with, then fifteen sprints from corner flag to corner flag. They specifically practised corner kicks, which Morgans always took. Taylor wanted the ball crossed hard into the penalty area at about nine feet high and they would train for hours getting the ball crossed and headed into goal.

As the only Welshman in the side, Murphy had a special liking for Morgans and always called him 'Dai'. Whenever Jimmy Murphy managed Wales and Kenny Morgans was playing, Murphy used to send Morgans out the room for the team talk because he knew Morgans had heard it all before and would only smirk at how horrified the other players were at his colourful language.

Morgans was the youngest member of the team at the time of the crash. He escaped with only minor injuries, but he lay unconscious for several days. Morgans lost heart after the crash. In all, he made only 23 first-team appearances in two and a half years for the club before joining Swansea and moving back to Wales. He played for his home team for a couple more seasons and then retired from football altogether.

David Pegg was born on 20th September 1935 and raised in Highfields, just north of Doncaster. Like Mark Jones, he was a Yorkshireman to the core. His father, Bill, was a 'banksman', the man responsible for the safety of the miners going to and from the coalface in cages. As a kid, Pegg used to buy his boot studs from Woolworth's in Doncaster and used to wear hand-knitted stockings. He played for Doncaster Boys and Yorkshire Boys at inside-left, but was put out on the left wing for an England Boys match. The left-half that day was Duncan Edwards.

Spotted by a United scout that day, Pegg signed for United in 1950, needing special permission from his headmaster to leave school early, and made his debut against Middlesbrough on 6th December 1952. Although he was right-handed, Pegg was left-footed, but could take corners with either foot.

He was one of the players whose standard of play was always very high and he worked particularly well with Dennis Viollet on the pitch. On one specific occasion, however, Pegg had a nightmare game. Just before a match against Tottenham Hotspur, Pegg had a huge injection for toothache, which made him extremely nauseous and dizzy. He needed help getting changed and two other players had to hold him up when they came out of the tunnel for the start of the game. He didn't look very clever on the pitch and, the first time he got the ball, he started running in the wrong direction.

Pegg had worked his way through the junior teams and had secured a place in United's first team with remarkable speed and assurance. He was always in competition with Albert Scanlon for the left-wing position, though according to Busby, Pegg was "our best left winger by a mile." A supremely confident player, he was hotly tipped to replace Tom Finney on the left wing for England and become an England regular, but Pegg only ever won one full cap, which his eight-year-old nephew wore while watching the 1974 World Cup.

Along with Eddie Colman and Tommy Taylor, Pegg was the player whose company everyone loved. He was always smiling and had time for anyone. Mrs Watson used to say to Billy Whelan, "Why don't you go out with David, Billy? David's great for a night out." After one particularly heavy Saturday night, unshaven and still reeking of drink, he and Colman hid in the toilets at Old Trafford on Sunday morning, waiting until Busby had left the ground. Busby came into the dressing rooms as he usually did and chatted to Tom Curry for a few minutes, then used the toilets. Just before he left to go home, Busby said to Tom Curry, "Tell Pegg and Colman they can come out of the toilets now."

Very good-looking and a sharp dresser, Pegg had a natural charm that women found irresistible. He had a great many girlfriends but, according to his sister Irene, he was "not a committer". He was just as happy in the company of men and he, Bobby Charlton and Tommy Taylor often used to go back to Pegg's parents' house where they would spend a few days fishing on the River Trent. Indeed, the Pegg family saw so much of Taylor that Pegg's sister took a shine to him, but it didn't last. At the time of the crash, the twenty-three-year-old Pegg was the only player who wasn't married or who didn't have a steady girlfriend.

The Pegg family heard about his death suddenly and rather brutally, before Jimmy Murphy had a chance to ring and tell them himself. The morning after the crash, the Peggs' doorbell rang at 7am. Irene answered the door and the policeman standing there said "Tha' David's dead, what dost want doing with t'body?" Irene Pegg continues: "After he died I thought for a while my mother was going to go mental. There were thousands at the funeral, and all these people in the house that no one knew. Policemen were directing traffic, the road was closed. It was as if the Queen were coming. It were awful. You're just there as a bystander, but he was my brother, not an international footballer... Someone still puts flowers on his grave. I know which flowers I put on and there is still someone leaves a flower on it. I'd love to know who it is..."

Albert Scanlon, an only child, was born in Hulme, Manchester, on 10th October 1935. Raised as a Catholic, his family were original Irish immigrants. He learnt to play football on the bomb-sites around Manchester. "In 1945, there was no football pitches in Hulme," Scanlon remembers, "except the barracks which was a bombed fire station at one end, a swimming baths at the other side, all demolished. There was no grass in Hulme, no grass at all. There was plenty of crofts. And sometimes, people had cleared the crofts, you know, like the one we used to play on at Leaf Street. It was a warehouse that had been blown down – it must have been half a mile long. But they put shingle on it, black shingle, so if you fell down you cut yourself. And the pubs used to have a Sunday league team – the White Horse or the Red Horse or something. And then there was Cooper's, Coopers were all Irish people, the Cheshire Cheese, the Seven Stars and then they had a schoolboy league side. But that pitch was a croft, as I say. To have a game of football on grass, schoolboys used to go to Gorton on buses to the park right opposite Belle Vue, and then you'd put two coats down and you'd have a football match."

When Scanlon was thirteen or so, the Captain of Manchester United, Johnny Carey, came to Scanlon's school to give a presentation. United had just won a famous FA Cup Final victory against Blackpool and the team was looked on with awe. In front of all his schoolmates, Scanlon was introduced to Carey, who asked him what his ambition was. Hulme, where Scanlon grew up, was Manchester City territory, so when Scanlon replied "To play for United", everyone laughed.

One of the original Babes, Scanlon's career at Manchester United is a classic example of the success of United's Youth Policy. Without costing the club a penny, Scanlon helped United win the Championship in 1956 and '57, scoring 35 goals in all. Scanlon played a very quick, direct game on the left wing, but he lacked David Pegg's flair and usually lost his place to Pegg. One of his greatest moments for United was the famous game against Arsenal at Highbury, just before the team left for Belgrade. United won 5–4 and Scanlon was named man of the match. For the game against Red Star, Scanlon was chosen over Pegg.

He was known by his team mates as 'Joe Friday' after the detective in *Dragnet*, the American television series, because he knew everything. Dennis Viollet once said to Scanlon: "Don't you ever, ever write a book till I'm dead. You know too much. Don't ever write a book Scanny." Of medium build with ginger hair and blue eyes, Scanlon was very good-looking as a young man. He married Josie, a beautician from Lewis's department store, when he was nineteen and went on to have four children with her.

According to Harry Gregg, Scanlon was afraid of Jimmy Murphy. Gregg says, "In a game we were playing, Albert in the first half would be playing outside left on the same side as the dugout where Jimmy would be and then in the second half because they changed round Albert would be the far side. Jimmy used to say to him, first half, 'I'll see you at halftime Scanlon, I'm telling you now, when you get to the other side, if you see an old man standing in the crowd calling you names with a hat on, it'll be bloody me.' They all loved Murphy, but Albert was shit scared of Jimmy."

At the crash site, Scanlon was found under a wheel, lying unconscious in the snow and was originally left for dead by the German rescuers. He suffered a fractured skull, but was out of hospital within a month. When he arrived back at Manchester's Victoria Station, he flagged down a cab and, when the cabbie realised who Scanlon was, he said Scanlon could use his taxi, free of charge, whenever he wished. Like Kenny Morgans, Scanlon's playing career at Manchester United after the crash was short-lived. He moved to Newcastle United in 1961 where he stayed for just one season, thence to Lincoln City and Mansfield Town. Scanlon stopped playing altogether in 1966 when he was just thirty-one years old. For the rest of his working life, Scanlon got a job on the Salford docks, where he was known as 'Pockets'.

Incredibly handsome, charming and athletic, Tommy Taylor was one of the main attractions of the Manchester United team. With his film-star good looks, he represented everything that was glamorous about the Busby Babes. Along with Roger Byrne and Duncan Edwards, he was the fittest player in the team, regularly training far more than the other players, although some have mischievously claimed this was necessary to keep his body trim as he was prone to putting on the pounds. As well as Byrne and Edwards, Taylor was a regular choice for England, and was set to replace Nat Lofthouse as the team's main striker. In all, he appeared nineteen times in an England shirt, scoring 16 goals.

Born on 29th January 1932, Taylor was from a large working class family in Barnsley. His grandfather played centre half for Barnsley St Peter's, as it was called then, and was once offered a trial with Wakefield Trinity, which was a big club in those days. On his way to the trial, he passed some friends in a pub who asked him in for a good-luck drink – Taylor's grandfather ended up on the pub floor and never made it to the trial.

Taylor grew up with three brothers and two sisters in a two-up, two-down that backed on to a pub, The Woodman, run by his aunt Hester. He and his friends used to play football for a local pit team on a piece of rock-hard ground called The Bog – it was here that he was spotted at fifteen by a Barnsley scout and signed by the club in 1947. He carried on playing for Barnsley reserves during his National Service in the Army. On Friday evenings, the Barnsley coach used to drive over to north Wales, where Taylor was stationed, and pick him up for the game on Saturday.

Taylor moved to Manchester United in March 1953, aged 21. The agreed signing fee was £30,000, but Busby didn't want to saddle Taylor with the pressure of a £30,000 price tag, so he paid £29,999 and gave an Old Trafford tea lady the remaining £1. Albert Scanlon met Taylor the day Taylor arrived at the club:

"So the following Tuesday I'm mopping the floor and the door opens in the dressing room and the boss walks in and Jimmy walks in, this big centre forward from Barnsley – he was a huge lad – and Walter Crickmer and Bert Whalley. So they introduced Tommy to Bill and Tom and me and he says, 'Tommy's just signed for us, centre forward'. So I'm mopping away and Jimmy says to me, 'What you doing tonight?' So I say, 'I'm gonna watch City and Rangers', they were playing in a friendly. You didn't see many Scottish teams and you all had a little book that would get you in any football ground, plus three cinemas in town or the opera house, so long as you phoned up. So he says, 'That's it' he says, 'take Tommy to Maine Road'. So I says, 'Where will I meet him?' So he says, 'Take him with you, to your mam's for his tea'. 'Oh' I said, 'alright'. So he says, 'You can go now, Bill'll finish that'. So we got on a bus, me and Tommy – just paid thirty thousand for him – walked down Medlock Street, went in and me mam was sat on a pouffe and she looked at this big fellow like that, and I says, 'This is Tommy, Tommy Taylor, he's just signed for United and Mr Murphy's asked me to take him to the match' – 'cos I didn't call him Jimmy, called him Mister – 'Mr Murphy's asked me to take him to the match and he wants his tea', you know. So she says, 'Oh. D'you eat fish, chips and peas?' and he says, 'Yeah'. She says, 'Well you can have that'. She says to me, 'Get a dish and go to Greasy Annie's' and Tommy sat down with a plate – fish, chips and peas – like me, tea, bread and butter and a mug of tea. And he had that and I took him to the match, walked him back, put him on a bus to where he was going and every Easter he sent me mam a box of chocolates, Tommy. Every Easter, there was no failing with it."

Taylor made his debut for United against Preston North End on 7th March 1953 and scored two goals, one of which was a header from outside the penalty area. Taylor was a very good header of the ball and a very strong finisher. By all accounts, he could head a ball more accurately than most could kick it. He was 'pin-toed' and it was said that he could murder a ball with either foot, but he was fairly clumsy dribbling with it. He partnered Dennis Viollet up front and this absolutely deadly partnership was one of the principle reasons for United's success during the Busby Babes era.

Taylor was one of those players for whom success curiously brought with it a great deal of criticism, hostility even. There was no particular reason why this should be the case for Taylor, but the more popular and successful he became, the more stick he took from fans and press in general, and from Henry Rose from the *Daily Express* in particular. Scanlon says, "Henry Rose was always slagging Tommy Taylor, always, and he interviewed him coming back from Prague. And he says to him, 'Why do you want to interview me, you're always slagging me?' And he says, 'Ah, but you're the one that sells papers Tommy'."

He liked his beer and, apparently, could polish off a dozen bottles of lager in one night and still train well the next morning. According to David Pegg's sister, he was a "gobby bugger" and vain, too. He once went into the local barbers to get out of the rain and told them to keep cutting his hair until it stopped. It rained for ages and, by the time it had stopped, his hair was so short he refused to take his hat off for days afterwards. Part of the Old Trafford Crazy Gang, Taylor was well known for his party antics and for his womanising, but at the time of the crash, he had settled down and was engaged to Norma Curtis. By the time of his death, Taylor had scored 112 goals in 168 first-team appearances for United, which is one goal every one and a half matches – an absolutely stunning goal rate.

The other player with an equally prodigious goal rate was Taylor's partner up front, Dennis Viollet. In 294 appearances for the club, Viollet scored 179 goals, a ratio not far off Taylor's. Assessing his impact as a forward, Busby said "Dennis was quicksilver, a wonderful chance-taker." Viollet could read the game superbly, spotting where a player was moving and slotting the ball into space for them. His touch on the ball was second to none. In Harry Gregg's opinion, Viollet was the best player in the side.

Like Roger Byrne, Albert Scanlon and Eddie Colman, Viollet was a local lad. Born on 20th September 1933, and raised in Manchester, he played for his school team and was spotted early, signing for Manchester United on 1st September 1949. It took Viollet longer than some to work his way through the junior and reserve teams and secure a first-team place, but he eventually did so, making his debut on 11th April 1953.

Viollet was known as 'Tricky Viollet' to his team mates, a nickname that alludes to his sinuous and complicated personality. Viollet was always very much his own man and never followed the crowd. He mixed with his team mates socially, as they all did, going out with them on Saturday nights to the Locarno or the Cromford Club, but he would often leave before the others, or else be the last to leave. He was a loner, slightly mistrustful. No one could ever be sure where he was exactly, or what he was up to. There were whole sides of him that remained hidden from his team mates.

He was also a notorious ladies' man. He loved the company of woman and knew how to treat them. Because of this unusually sophisticated side to his personality, women were incredibly attracted to him. Indeed, he met his first wife, Barbara, when he was just seventeen. She quickly became pregnant by him and they married. Their son, Roger, was named after Roger Byrne. Married life, however, didn't stop Viollet living like a bachelor and he developed a particular passion for Jewish girls. A year after the crash, Scanlon took Viollet to an evening organised by the Jewish Association. "I introduced Dennis to Helen, I met Helen when she was sixteen. Jewish girl, long red hair, in an emerald green dress and the chap that was running the dance said, 'Don't bother Albert, she's only sixteen'. She danced up the floor towards me, without shoes on, and I introduced her to Dennis and that started it, Dennis divorced his missus and married her."

Relatively speaking, Viollet was not too badly hurt in the air crash and was discharged from the hospital in Munich three weeks afterwards. He returned to England by train with Kenny Morgans. Life took on a different quality for Viollet after Munich – he seemed to want to lead as full a life as possible from then on. With nearly all the friends he had grown up with either dead or shipped off to other clubs, Viollet started nightclubbing regularly with some of the younger players in the side, his favourite haunt being the Continental club, where he would stay until the early hours. Busby was not impressed, but Viollet continued to play well, scoring 32 goals in 36 games during the 1959/60 season – a tally that remains the club record. A stalemate ensued until, eventually, the inevitable happened and Busby informed Viollet in 1961 that he was being sold to Stoke City. Once again, Busby made sure his wishes prevailed. Viollet stayed at Stoke until 1967, playing alongside Stanley Matthews, and had a very successful second career at the club, which gave him a testimonial in his final season. Viollet died in 1999.

Liam Wheelan was born on 1st April 1935 into a large, close-knit Working class family in Cabra, Dublin. His father, John, was a time-keeper at a local factory and died of TB when Whelan was just seven. Devoutly Catholic throughout his short life, Whelan was a non-drinker and a non-smoker and, as an adolescent, thought seriously about becoming a priest. He grew up playing football in the streets of Cabra and played for the Republic of Ireland Schoolboys team that beat England Schoolboys 8-4. He went on to be selected for Dublin's famous Home Farm club, which was the breeding ground for Ireland's most famous footballers. Whelan was also an accomplished hurling player. He was picked to play for Dublin for both the football and hurling teams on the same day, but chose to pursue football.

In the spring of 1953, Bert Whalley was in Ireland to sign a young Home Farm player called Vinnie Ryan.

Billy Behan, United's chief Irish scout, took Whalley to the game to watch Ryan, but the player who caught Whalley's eye that day was not Ryan, but Whelan, who had a very good game indeed. So impressed was Whalley that he took the unusual step of offering him a contract there and then. Whelan was eighteen. Nine days after being bought, he made his debut against Wolves in the first leg of the FA Youth Cup Final in 1953. United won 7-1, a terrific scoreline that including a goal from Whelan. He scored 26 goals in 39 matches in the championship winning season of 1956/57, and a total of 43 goals in 79 Division One matches.

For a midfielder, this was a terrific strike rate. Whelan was an inside forward, playing just behind Tommy Taylor and alongside Dennis Viollet. Although he could sometimes look clumsy on the ball, he had the knack of 'ghosting' his opponents – leaving them standing by feigning going one way only to go the other. Whelan could never outrun players, but what he lacked in pace, he more than made up for in terms of deftness and natural ability. He was so skilful on the ball that, when Whelan played in a youth tournament in Switzerland, United were approached by a Brazilian club to buy him. One of Whelan's trademarks was the nutmeg. Before one of his two international games against England, Duncan Edwards bet Whelan that he couldn't do it to him. During the game, Whelan got the ball on the touchline and sure enough, when Edwards came to tackle, he nutmegged him.

Deeply homesick for Ireland, Whelan never really settled in Manchester. He went out little and sent his mother £3 every week as he had no need of money. Whelan was great friends with Bobby Charlton, at one time sharing a room at Mrs Watson's lodging house with him, but eventually he lost his place in the side to him. Otherwise, he was very shy and retiring – most of his acquaintances in Manchester were Irish priests. So uncomfortable with fame was he that, whenever he wore his United blazer, he used to carry a raincoat over his arm to hide the badge. According to Busby, Whelan had an inferiority complex. During one particular game at Old Trafford, the crowd started jibing Whelan for his lazy style. Whelan subsequently asked Busby to be left out of the team because, he said, "they are all having a go at me." Busby replied: "Worry when I have a go at you, son."

He didn't play in the game in Belgrade and apparently was not well at the time of the trip. Famously said "Well, if it happens, I'm ready to go" moments before the crash. He was just twenty-two. Jimmy Murphy told Whelan's mother the bad news himself. The Whelans didn't have a phone, so Murphy had to ring friends of the family two doors down. Some time after the crash, Harry Gregg saw Whelan's mother and told her what his last words were, which was a source of great comfort to the family. After Whelan died, his mother received a letter from a priest in Spain telling her that Whelan used to send old shirts and other mementos to the boys in his seminary. No one in his family knew anything about this. Without any fuss, without drawing attention to himself, it was just the kind of thing Whelan would do.

Ray Wood, known as 'Woody', or 'Puffer', because he always had a fag in his mouth, was born on 11th June 1931 in County Durham. He was bought from Doncaster in the summer of 1950 for £6,000 when he was eighteen-years-old. His style of play was limited – all he did was stay on the goal line and stop shots. When he was a boy in the North-East, he won a medal for his sprinting and almost became a professional sprinter, so quick was he off the line. He couldn't deal with crosses very well, though. Some didn't rate him at all. Tom Curry said that if a bale of hay went past him he wouldn't be able to catch it. Jackie Blanchflower told him he was the second worst goalkeeper he ever saw. "Who's the worst?" was all that Wood said.

After the Munich aircrash, he never managed to regain the first team place he had lost to Harry Gregg, although the two remained life-long friends, and he was moved on to Huddersfield Town, where he stayed for several years. After retiring from football, he took on coaching appointments in America, Canada, Greece, Kuwait, the UAE and Zambia and managed the national sides of Cyprus and Kenya. He died in 2002.

In May 1954, Manchester United took its squad of youth players to Zurich to take part in a tournament hosted by a Zurich youth team called Blue Stars. This was the first time that any English club had taken part in a competition of this kind. Busby felt that participation in the competition was vital for his young players – they would be put under a different kind of pressure and it would expand their game. The club, too, attached a great deal of importance to the tournament, so much so that James Gibson, the Chairman, joined Busby, Murphy and Bert Whalley on the trip.

Among the players who participated in the tournament were Bobby Charlton, Eddie Colman, Duncan Edwards, Dave Pegg, Albert Scanlon and Billy Whelan. For many, if not all, of the boys, it was their first trip abroad. They arrived in Zurich and were put up at Hotel Stoller, a four-star hotel in the middle of the city. Everything was new. There were trams, rolling along on the wrong side of the street. Lettuce on a side plate, not on the main plate. There were wooden shutters on the windows. And how did duvets work? Where were the sheets?

The following morning, they played three matches, twenty minutes each way, with the final in the afternoon. They played

Blue Stars, Young Fellows, both from Zurich and a team from
Berne. Manchester United won. After the tournament finished,
Busby took the boys on a little holiday to Interlaken and then
on to Berne, where they played a friendly. The whole trip
lasted seven days and was a real education for the young boys.
They had to cope with completely different styles of play and
came across the 'sweeper' system for the first time.

They returned to Zurich in 1955 to defend their title and
won the tournament again. In 1956, they went again, but this
time the competition included teams from Italy, Germany
and Yugoslavia and wasn't quite as easy as it had been before.
United got through to the final, but lost 1-0 to Genoa. The
Italian side only came out of their own half once, which
was when they managed to score. They then sat back and let
United come at them, but the boys from Manchester couldn't
break through. They were exposed for the first time to the
classic Italian game.

Ever since he had seen the Hungarians beat England in
1953, Busby was convinced that the Hungarians' 'new style'
was the way forwards for his young team. He wasn't seeking
to copy the Hungarians' game, but he wanted the players
to learn how to cope with European styles of play. Busby
knew the experience of playing against European teams was
incalculable for these young players. Unbeknownst to them,
or Busby, at the time, they would have to draw on this new
experience very soon indeed, since Manchester United were
about to start their great adventure in European football by
taking part in a brand new football competition, one that had
been cooked up in the offices of a French sports paper – the
European Cup.

4

EUROPE

I n September 1956, the League Champions, Manchester United, became the first English club ever to play competitive football in Europe. The new competition, set up in 1955 by the French sports paper *L'Equipe*, was impressively called the 'European Champions' Cup'. The French paper proposed that the Champions from sixteen European nations should play in a knock-out competition to decide the best team in Europe. But although United were the first English team to compete in Europe, they were not the first to be asked. The previous year's champions, Chelsea, had been invited to participate in the inaugural year of the competition, but the Football League Management Committee heaped pressure on the club not to take part, saying that the English League programme was above all other considerations. Chelsea backed down.

The English game at that time was still highly insular. The feeling within football's governing bodies was that the game in England was too hard for the continentals to handle. But more than this, there was a latent xenophobia built into the governing system. Alan Hardaker, Chairman of the Football League, was once quoted as saying: "I don't like Europe. Too many wops and dagoes!" As an English invention, many in the game felt it should remain being played the English way.

Matt Busby, however, did not agree. The Hungarian side of 1953 was the kind of football he liked and he saw European football as part of the dream he had for Manchester United. Considering *L'Equipe*'s invitation at a board meeting in May 1956, the chairman of the club, Harold Hardman, asked Busby whether it was wise to take on the extra commitments that European football would require, to which Busby replied, with admirable open-mindedness and prescience, that football was no longer a solely English phenomenon. The world was getting smaller, air travel was getting easier – the future of football lay outside the British Isles. "All right," said Hardman, "let's just try it."

The FA, its nose put out of joint by United's decision, retaliated by making life as difficult as possible for the club. They told the team that they would have to make sure to arrive back in the country from any European fixture at least 24 hours before the kick-off time for their next league game or else face some unnamed punitive measures – some points docked, perhaps. This threat meant that United's schedule was frantic when they played abroad. After the league match on the Saturday, the players would fly out on the Monday, play their match on Wednesday and then hurry back on Thursday to recover in time for the match on Saturday. It was a pattern that was followed year in, year out, for many years to come.

On Wednesday 12th September 1956, United began their long and famous European campaign by playing Anderlecht in Brussels in the preliminary round of the European Cup. For the trip to Brussels, neither Duncan Edwards, Eddie Colman nor Bobby Charlton was available because they were doing their National Service. Although the Army allowed them to play for United at weekends, they were not allowed to during the week. Despite this setback, however, United still won 2-0, with goals from Viollet and Taylor. At great expense, four huge sets of floodlights were in the process of being installed in Old Trafford. This new-fangled idea would allow the club to draw crowds for midweek Wednesday evening games – thus earning precious revenue – as well as not having to start matches early on Saturday afternoons during the winter months. But, because the floodlights at Old Trafford were not yet ready to be used, the second leg against Anderlecht had to be played at Maine Road.

Two weeks later, a crowd of 43,635 people stood in the rain to watch United demolish Anderlecht 10-0, with four goals from Dennis Viollet, three from Tommy Taylor, two from Billy Whelan and one from Johnny Berry. Man of the match, however, was Jackie Blanchflower – a late replacement for Duncan Edwards, who had injured himself at the weekend. The result still ranks as United's greatest margin of victory in Europe. The Anderlecht captain, Mermans, was extremely gracious in defeat: "The best teams of Hungary have never beaten us like this," he said, "They are fantastic. They should pick this whole team for England." This would almost have been possible, since only Billy Whelan and Jackie Blanchflower were not eligible for selection for England. Busby described the evening as "the finest exhibition of teamwork I have ever seen from any team, club or international. It was as near perfect football as anyone could wish to see."

In the next round, United were drawn against Borussia Dortmund. Word had got around after the match against Anderlecht and an astonishing 75,598 people came to Maine Road to see United play their first leg on Wednesday 17th October. They began well, scoring three goals in thirty-five minutes, but Dortmund were tougher opposition than Anderlecht and pulled two goals back. The game ended 3-2 to United. The return leg five weeks later ended in a goalless draw and so United were through thanks to their defence in general and Mark Jones in particular.

Next came Atlético Bilbao in the quarter-finals. The first leg was away and the idea of flying to Bilbao to play a football match was a new and alien prospect for the players. Few had been further afield than Bolton or Bradford, let alone as exotic a place as Bilbao, and no one had been on a plane before. It ended up being a pretty awful journey for the players. Billy Whelan was dreadfully ill on board and Bill Foulkes accidentally turned off the heating with his feet, leaving everyone shivering and cold.

The weather in Bilbao was terrible and, far from being exotic, the conditions in the football stadium were atrocious. After heavy rain and snow, the pitch was more of a swamp than a playing field. United went 3-0 down very quickly, but managed to pull two goals back in the second half. Then Bilbao scored two more goals, "silly goals" as Busby described them. Suddenly, a three-goal deficit looked insurmountable. But then Billy Whelan scored one of the most celebrated goals in United's history. Picking the ball up in his own half, he sauntered through the Spanish defence, beating one man after another, none of whom seemed to know quite what to do. Whelan continued up field, gathering pace all the time until he got to the edge of the penalty area. Everyone expected a shot, but Whelan carried on into the penalty area, drawing the Spanish keeper off his line. Now Whelan picked his spot, placing his right-footed shot into the top left-hand corner. It was an absolutely exquisite individual effort. Suddenly, 5-3 with the home leg to come didn't seem to be quite so bad.

The following morning, the weather was still terrible and the Dakota due to take the team home was snow-bound at the airport. Well aware that they would have the FA on their backs if United missed their forthcoming home game against Sheffield Wednesday, everything was done to try to get the plane in the air. Bill Foulkes, along with Colman, Charlton and Duncan Edwards, climbed onto the wings with brushes and swept the snow off. And it wasn't just the players who mucked in – the press, officials and airport staff helped to get the plane ready for take-off. The weather remained bad as they left Bilbao, but as they approached the Channel Islands, where they would stop to refuel, the weather became bright and sunny. As the plane descended towards Jersey airport, however, the plane appeared to be alarmingly short of the runway and, much to the players' horror, seemed to be dropping into the sea. Realising his error, the captain opened the engines and the plane rose again, over the cliffs and fields, eventually making a safe landing. It was, Johnny Berry said, "a close thing."

Back in Manchester, the Old Trafford floodlights were frustratingly still not ready, so the return leg against Bilbao was again played at Maine Road. More than 70,000 people attended the game on 6th February 1957. Bilbao had come to Manchester with only one thing in mind – to protect their lead. They pulled every player back into defence and so everyone watching was fully expecting a very dull game indeed. They couldn't have been more wrong. For those who saw it, the game that night is still classed as one of the most thrilling of United's history in European football.

United were unbelievable in the ferociousness of their attack, and it soon paid off. Just before half-time, Duncan Edwards surged up field and let loose one of his trademark cannon shots. The famous Spanish defender, Garay, stopped the ball with his leg, but the ball landed at Dennis Viollet's feet, who punted it in. After half-time, United didn't let up at all, with Viollet scoring again within minutes. The whistle blew, but the German referee was blowing for offside, not to award the goal. No one could believe it. A moment later, Billy Whelan scored and the crowd went wild, but the referee once again blew for offside. Both these decisions turned Maine Road into a cauldron of whistles and jeers. Bobby Charlton, missing the game because of National Service, was nonetheless in the crowd that night and has said that he seldom experienced such a charged atmosphere.

The teams stayed locked in a stalemate until the seventieth minute, when Tommy Taylor, hitting the post just minutes before, swerved past Garay and blasted the ball into the net with his left foot. This time, the referee awarded the goal. The teams were now level on aggregate with twenty minutes left on the clock. Bilbao were reeling from the shock but managed to keep United out. With five minutes to go, Tommy Taylor found himself with the ball out on the right wing with Garay on his heels. He found the extra space to go round Garay and, with Johnny Berry screaming for it on the edge of the box, Taylor gently rolled the ball back to him. Berry thumped it into the back of the net, sending the crowd into paroxysms. On the touchline, the chimney-smoking Matt Busby started leaping up and down and Jimmy Murphy openly wept, later describing the game as "my greatest game in football." United were through, 3-0 on the night and 6-5 on aggregate. The 'Red Devils', as they had recently been called by the press, left the field to an ecstatic ovation. The United fans had simply never before seen their team pass such an intense examination of their abilities with such flying colours. Bilbao's captain, Piru Gainza, said: "They play with such passion we were simply overwhelmed."

United's semi-final opponents were Real Madrid, the European Cup holders. Busby had flown to Nice to watch them and came back full of admiration for the Spaniards. Their Argentine striker, Alfredo di Stéfano – the greatest player in the world – was nicknamed the 'White Arrow'; their left winger, Gento, was a legend; while forwards Raymond Kopa,

Mateos and Rial completed a formidable and intimidating line-up. Madrid's halfback line – the captain Muñóz, Marcos 'Marquitos' Alonso and Zárraga – were just as formidable. Normally, Busby didn't concentrate on the opposition's strong points just before a game as he felt that this would not be good for his own players' confidence, but this time the opposition was Real Madrid, and so he broke his usual rule. He passed on to the players all the tips he had gathered from watching Real's game, but he tried to prepare Bill Foulkes in particular, warning him of Gento's speed down that left wing. "He can run, Bill, he can run," Busby said.

The first leg at the Bernabeu Stadium on 11th April was watched by a staggering 130,000 people. Busby was spot on about Gento – he was so quick and skilful that Bill Foulkes did not touch the ball once during the whole game. Soon, United were 2-0 down and, though Tommy Taylor scored to make it 2-1, Real scored again to win the game 3-1. As expected, di Stéfano was the game's main playmaker, but Jackie Blanchflower had a good game against him. At one point, Blanchflower coolly took the ball of di Stéfano and fed the ball forward quickly and cleverly. Di Stéfano was less than pleased and gave Blanchflower a nasty kick on the backs of his heels. Bill Foulkes waded in, pushing di Stéfano in the back and glowering at him. Di Stéfano raised his hands in apology and walked away.

Although United's first few games in Europe were not covered by the English press, United had captured the nation's imagination so completely that pressmen were now being flown out to watch these thrilling away games. On this particular occasion, defeat tasted bitter and the by-line in the *Daily Herald* the next day was "Murder in Madrid". The paper sprang to United's defence, claiming that the Spaniards had fouled their way through the match. Tommy Taylor, in particular, had been targeted. The Spanish defence was so nervous of Taylor's abilities in the air that the only way they could contain him, the paper claimed, was to hold him round the waist and drag him down every time he jumped. The simple truth, however, is that the Spaniards played a game too wily for the young bucks.

The floodlighting at Old Trafford had finally been finished and so the return leg against Real Madrid was the first ever home game in European competition. The brightly-lit stage was set for a gripping encounter. After coming back from behind against Atlético Bilbao, the 60,000 plus crowd was fully expectant that the team could do it again. United started the game in their usual high-tempo style, flooding into Real's half time and again, but the Madrid defence was rock solid. Then, after half an hour, Old Trafford was stunned into silence as Kopa scored against the run of play. A few minutes later, di Stefano scored again for Real and United were suddenly four goals adrift. The job now looked like a very tall order indeed, even by their standards. Despite goals from Tommy Taylor and Bobby Charlton, the task did indeed prove to be insurmountable – 2- 2 on the night, Real Madrid going through 5-3 on aggregate. It was a hard lesson for the team – feted in England, they were simply outplayed and outclassed by the best side in Europe. They would have to smarten up in future. "It was a contest between two great teams," Busby said afterwards, "a mature side and a young side and, of course, experience told. But our time will come."

Although United's European dream was over, for now, they were still in with a chance of doing the double at home, a feat no team had managed since Aston Villa in 1897. They were top of the League and, within a few weeks of losing to Real Madrid, United were crowned League Champions for the second year running after a 1-1 draw at home against West Bromwich Albion. Keeping alive the hopes for the double, they reached the FA Cup Final as well, where they would meet

Aston Villa. An FA Cup Final at Wembley is always a proud moment for a manager, but Busby was especially proud of his squad. In no time at all, Roger Byrne and the boys had won two league titles and were now in their first FA Cup Final, the first of many, Busby hoped.

On 4th May, Wembley was full to brimming when the whistle blew for the kick-off, but within six minutes, disaster struck. Peter McParland, the Villa left-winger, had gone into the box to chase his own header, one that had been easily collected by the keeper Ray Wood, when Wood, not seeing him, turned his head into McParland's shoulder charge. A sharp crack resounded around the stadium charge and Wood fell immediately to the ground. McParland went down too, but it was quickly obvious that Wood was the one who was seriously hurt. The crowd and the United players were incensed. The challenge was both reckless and unnecessary. Duncan Edwards stood threateningly over McParland and had to be calmed down by the captain, Roger Byrne. Wood was stretchered off and, because there were no substitutes in those days, it was eventually decided that Jackie Blanchflower would put on the keeper's green shirt. Duncan Edwards filled in at centre-half and Liam Whelan had to drop back to left-half.

After examining Wood, United's physio, Ted Dalton, announced to Busby that Wood had a depressed fracture of the cheekbone and was suffering from concussion. Busby told him to try to get Wood well enough to go back on. In the physio's room under the Wembley stands, Dalton tried shooting a few balls at Wood, but Wood could hardly see the ball, let alone stop it. It was no good. Desperate to come back on and help his team mates, however, Wood went into the car park where he kicked a ball around with a young boy in order to try to clear his vision. For the remainder of the first half, United hung on valiantly and went into the break 0-0. Busby knew he needed eleven players on the pitch and so it was agreed that Wood would come back on in the second half, but not in goal – he would stay out of harm's way on the wing and would only return in goal if he felt able to stop shots. For 75 minutes, the score remained 0-0, but then McParland scored. Eight minutes later, McParland scored again and, in a desperate last flurry of activity, Byrne waved Wood back into goal and the team assumed its normal shape. The last seven or eight minutes were all United. Edwards went on the rampage and, with three minutes, crossed the ball in to Tommy Taylor, who was there waiting for it. He headed the ball in and suddenly it was 2-1 with all to play for. United created more chances in the dying minutes of the game, but Villa managed to hold out for their controversial victory.

As a postscript to that game, there are two stories that exemplify and typify the differences in attitude and approach between Murphy and Busby. As League Champions and FA Cup Holders respectively, United and Villa met again at Old Trafford at the start of the following season for the Charity Shield, a match everyone knew would be fraught because of the ill-feeling the Cup Final had generated. Busby was having none of it, though, and insisted that, before kick-off, Ray Wood would meet McParland in the centre circle and shake his hand. The matter was best forgotten, Busby said. Wood did what Busby instructed. Murphy's response, however, was to take Bill Foulkes aside before the game and tell him to give McParland some stick. As soon as he could, Foulkes went in hard and knocked McParland off the pitch and on to the cinder track. Murphy shouted: "I wanted you to wait until he'd got the ball, Billy!"

Despite the frustration of losing the Cup Final in such unjust circumstances and missing out on the glorious double, Busby could once again enter his Championship-winning side into the European Cup, a competition that was beginning to obsess him. In Paris for the European Cup draw, Busby was approached by representatives from Real Madrid asking him if he would like to manage the club. The offer came as a complete surprise to Busby and he was hugely flattered, of course, but he turned them down. Manchester United was still very much a work-in-progress for Busby and nothing would deter him from his dream of further and greater achievements for his players.

United were drawn against Shamrock Rovers in the opening round. On 25th September 1957, United travelled to Billy Whelan's hometown of Dublin, where the amateurs were trounced 6-0, with Whelan himself scoring twice. It was David Pegg, though, who scored the best goal on the night. Picking up a cross-field pass from Duncan Edwards, Pegg had only the keeper to beat from twenty-five yards. The keeper ran Pegg down but, remaining calm, Pegg stood still and, with a controlled flick, floated the ball over the keeper's head and into the far corner. The crowd had never seen a goal quite like it.

Shamrock Rovers proved sterner opposition for the return leg at Old Trafford, but although Rovers narrowly lost 3-2, there was never a real doubt that United wouldn't progress. Next up were the Czechoslovakian champions, Dukla Prague, a team composed of soldiers who played at a ground called the Army Stadium. On 20th November, United beat Dukla comfortably 3-0 at home, with goals from Yorkshiremen Taylor and Pegg, but Busby knew that Dukla would be a much tougher proposition away. The Czechoslovakian authorities wanted to be seen as good hosts to these famous footballers; at the same time, however, they wanted to keep an eye on these Westerners, so much so that on every level of their hotel, there was a settee at either end of the corridor on which a fully-armed Czechoslovakian soldier sat and kept watch. Albert Scanlon takes up the story: "They took us to the pictures the first day and it was, you know the old little square screen like that window, that's how they was. And we pulled up at this cinema and we was there about ten minutes and what they were doing – we didn't know this at the time – they was clearing the first twenty rows out and the film had started and it was Bing Crosby, *Going My Way* and they cleared the first twenty rows out and then we went in and we sat from them, but they made sure there was a gap between us and the people that were in, you know, you weren't allowed to talk to 'em."

As you might expect of a military team, Dukla were well-drilled, neat and very tidy and two weeks later they beat United 1-0. The Busby Babes never liked losing, but at least they were through 3-1 on aggregate. Eddie Colman, in particular, was superb in Prague and was named man of the match. Scanlon says: "And we had this sort of a banquet, they all do, like United used to have theirs at the Midland. The orchestra was all women, you know, drums and violins and whatever else, so somebody says can we sing and one of the interpreters was called Peck, Beck or something – 'cos we had more interpreters when you went to one of them countries than you had players – and this Mr Beck says to us, 'I'll tell you the songs that are banned'. *It's a Long Way to Tipperary*, *Pack up your Troubles*, *Roll Out the Barrel* – all banned. So Eddie Colman on the drums, Mark, Tommy, David, Billy, Blanchy, all finished up on the stage singing *It's a Long Way to Tipperary* and the orchestra walked off, 'cos it was banned. But they wouldn't stop us. So this couple was sat on this table – and how they got there, we never know 'cos it was supposed to be a private banquet – she was a lovely girl and she was with this fellow. Tom [Curry] had asked us to take things with us like bacon, tins of beans, spaghetti, toothpaste, toothbrushes, razor blades, ladies nylons if you wanted, chocolate. And me and Tom Jackson [*Manchester Evening News* reporter], we always had Players Medium or Senior Service 'cos we'd get 'em on the planes, and we'd offer this girl one and she'd smoke it, but the fellow took one and he kept sticking it in his top pocket. So in the end Tom says, you know, 'What's that with the top pocket?' So he says, 'My papa'. So he says, 'Well, don't you smoke?' He says, 'Yeah, but my papa, English cigarettes'. So he says, 'Smoke 'em'. So he says to me, 'What have you got left in your room?' He said, 'Have you got cigs?' I said, 'Yeah, and chocolate'. So he says, 'I've got toothpaste and razor blades'. So we went upstairs and we brought these down and we're talking to 'em through the night and they keep looking at these four hundred cigarettes and we said, 'No, no, they're yours', and the chocolate and all. So we got out of them that they'd been engaged seven or eight years and they'd just been notified that week that they'd got a one room flat, so they were celebrating [that] they could get married. I mean I don't know how many else was in the flat. So it got to about twelve o'clock and we were going out anyway, they allowed us out, but we was going to the British Embassy. And we got up, shook our hands like, you know, and we're waiting around. And he got up and he put his mac on and his scarf, and she's still sat there. So Tom says to him, 'You forgot your young lady' and he went, 'No, no'. He says, 'Yeah, you forgot your young lady, you know, she's with you'. And he said, 'No' he says, 'for the cigarettes and chocolates you can have her for the night'. And I says, 'And she's agreeable?' So he says, 'For the cigarettes and chocolate, for the night'. Anyway, we turned it down and the next morning they shouted, 'Mr Scanlon, you're wanted' and I went to the coach door and she give me two boxes and I took 'em back and there was one like, Mr Jackson and Mr Scanlon and it was all cut glass. Well they're the best in the world at cut glass and this Mr Beck says to us, 'You must have give 'em something'. So we said, 'No, we just give 'em some chocolates and cigarettes while we were smoking'. We didn't tell 'em we'd give 'em like the four hundred cigarettes and the toothpaste, we just says we give 'em cigs when we were smoking. He said, 'Because you've got two months' wages there.' And she'd brought us 'em this early morning, brought 'em to the bus for me and Tom."

With the difficult job done in Prague, the journey home the following day was to prove a little more hazardous. Fog in London had delayed their BEA Viscount flight back to England. The players paced around the airport – Albert Scanlon and Tom Jackson with their cut crystal under their arms – but the fog showed no signs of clearing. All other flights out of Prague were heavily booked and it suddenly seemed that the team might not make it back in time for their league game against Birmingham City, thus incurring the wrath of Alan Hardaker. United's presence in Europe was still being met with a huge amount of resistance from the Football League and they continued to put pressure on United in the hope of preventing United from taking any further part in the competition. The issue was a huge headache for Busby and one he wanted to avoid aggravating at all costs.

After a great deal of to-ing and fro-ing, seats were eventually found for the players on a KLM flight bound for Amsterdam. From there, they caught a train to the Hook of Holland, a boat to Harwich, from there to London by train and then a train to Manchester. By the time Busby got the team back home, he was extremely relieved but everyone was absolutely exhausted. Busby and Walter Crickmer agreed that such a nightmarish journey should never happen again and so it was decided that from then on, for games deep in the heart of Europe, the club would hire a private charter plane to get the team there and back in relative comfort.

Their next opponents in Europe were Red Star Belgrade, but the first leg wasn't until 14th January, so the team had some time to relax and recuperate. In the meantime, the busy domestic schedule continued apace, but although the team was still grinding out the results, Busby felt they were not playing well, particularly in attack, and he decided to give his first team a real shake-up. For the match against Leicester City on 21st December, Busby dropped no fewer than five first team players – all internationals – and brought in some of the younger players clamouring to get into the first XI. Out went Johnny Berry, Liam Whelan and Dave Pegg and in came Ken Morgans, Bobby Charlton and Albert Scanlon. Jackie Blanchflower was also dropped in favour of Mark Jones and Harry Gregg made his debut for the club, replacing Ray Wood. To pull out five famous, first-team regulars and put in some newcomers and relative unknowns was unheard of at the time, but it was a policy Busby employed throughout the whole of his career as manager of United: "If they're good enough, they're old enough". This early version of the rotation system kept every player on his toes since the amount of time you'd been at the club made no difference to your chances of being picked. A team was selected for each match according to the demands of that particular game, not the needs or demands of the players. By now, the players knew Busby's system well enough and had no choice but to accept his decisions. It did the trick – United demolished Leicester City 4-0 and the new-look formation settled into a good run.

The Christmas and New Year campaign went well and then Busby had Red Star Belgrade to think about. Like Dukla, they were a hard team, well-organised and difficult to beat. Every player in their side was an international. Their goalkeeper, Beara, who used to be a ballet dancer and who was nicknamed the 'Black Cat', was widely thought to be the best keeper in the world. Busby had heard great things about one of their players in particular, the little inside-left, Sekularac, another master playmaker in the same vein as Hungary's Puskás. And then there was Tasic, their inside-left, who scored as many goals as any of United's strikers.

On the night of the first leg, Old Trafford was foggy and the stadium was again packed, the crowd in suspense for another great European fixture. European football was now something of a glamour-event in Manchester and the locals flocked to see these teams from far-off lands.

The game was evenly matched for the first half an hour, but the 35th minute brought what everyone in the stadium was dreading – a goal from Red Star. Tasic saw that Harry Gregg was off his line and lobbed him from 30 yards out. It was a sensational goal. From then on, Red Star closed ranks and shut up shop. They brought everyone back behind the ball and it was United who had to make all the play. Colman and Edwards tried repeatedly to open up Red Star's defence, but Beara was more than a match for them, pushing two certain goals round the post. On a rare break, Sekularac robbed Edwards of the ball in midfield and went forwards. Edwards was incensed – no one stole the ball from Duncan Edwards – and chased after Sekularac. When he caught up with him, he went in with a shoulder charge, got the ball back and sent Sekularac tumbling. Edwards' on-field presence that night was described by one reporter as like "a big red fire engine". Sitting on the ground, Sekularac was badly shaken and he didn't take any real part in the rest of the game.

The deadlock was finally broken in the 63rd minute, when Scanlon's cross was put past Beara by Bobby Charlton. As a relative newcomer to the team, Bobby Charlton was getting better with every game, proving Busby's decision to put him in the first team as a good one. Each of these European games was unknown territory and a real adventure for the United players, but Charlton showed no nerves, playing them as though he were still in the Eccles League.

Still United pressed. With ten minutes to go, yet another cross came into Red Star's box. On the end of this one was Eddie Colman, who stuck it into the net from eight yards away. It was one of the two goals that Eddie ever scored for the first team and, in light of how the Belgrade leg turned out, one of the most valuable any United player would ever score. Busby had said before the game that he wanted to go to Belgrade with a two-goal lead. The eventual margin of victory was not quite what Busby was hoping for, but at least it was a victory. If it hadn't been for Red Star's keeper, United would have had a bagful more.

The team had a few weeks before the return leg in Belgrade, during which time the players could rest and the club could organise their private aircraft to take them behind the Iron Curtain. Before that game, however, United had tricky opposition in the league, in the shape of Arsenal away at Highbury. By all accounts, this game, played just two days before United flew to Belgrade, was one of the greatest football matches ever seen on an English pitch. An event which heightened the drama and made the occasion more poignant for United was the fact that, the night before the match, one of the club's directors, George Whittaker, had died of a heart attack in his bed at the hotel.

Harry Gregg remembers: "When I got up in the middle of the night at the Lancaster Gate Hotel to go to the toilet, because you didn't have en suites in those days, no matter how big a star you were, and went out of the door and there was two policemen standing at the door next to me. I went back into the room again and thought, phew, something going on out there. Woke up the following morning, found out that the game would possibly be off because Mr George Whittaker had died in the middle of the night."

In the end, it was decided to carry on with the game. More than 63,000 poured into Highbury that day to watch the match. Busby kept the new arrivals in the side that had beaten Belgrade, and with Colman and Edwards supporting from their positions in midfield, the seven-man attack was

too much for Arsenal to handle. Within ten minutes, it was
Morgans who created the opening goal. Not yet nineteen
and revelling in his first spell in the team, Morgans weaved
his way through the left flank of the Arsenal defence before
picking out the onrushing Duncan Edwards who drove the
ball past the Arsenal keeper and into the back of the net
without breaking stride.

The outstanding player for United that day, however, was
Albert Scanlon, who made three of the five goals that day. On
the half hour, a lightning-quick raid down the left wing saw
Scanlon burst clear and cross the ball for Bobby Charlton,
who smashed it into the back of the net in his inimitable
style. Scanlon's raids down the left wing continued to send
Arsenal into panic and, just before half time, another of his
crosses switched the ball from left wing to Morgans on the
right, who then returned into the middle for Tommy Taylor
to sweep home. At half time, United left the field happy with
a 3-0 lead. This was proving to be one of United's greatest
exhibitions of attacking football, but back in the dressing
room, captain Roger Byrne was not at all happy. With Busby
and Murphy looking on in stunned silence, Byrne laid into
his team, saying that the game wasn't over, that the defence
had been sloppy and to brighten up. It's a measure of Byrne's
leadership qualities and ability to read the game that he was
spot on in his analysis.

The second half began, somewhat inevitably, in a more
subdued fashion. Arsenal had made some tactical changes
and switched their inside-forwards around and, just as all the
excitement of the first half seemed to have been drained out
of the afternoon, the game suddenly exploded into life with
an incredible burst of scoring by the home side. After fifteen
minutes, Arsenal scored three times in three minutes to draw
level and the home fans started baying for more. United were
totally rattled by this sudden onslaught but it was a measure of

their spirit that, rather than collapse and fold, they responded in the way they had been taught to play – by looking to score more goals of their own. The game opened up and United pressed on. It was from another of Scanlon's left wing centres that Viollet restored United's lead with the kind of hang-in-the-air header usually scored by Tommy Taylor. Five minutes later, Taylor produced a stunning goal of his own, running to the corner flag and somehow managing to get past a defender and into the box from where he drove the ball past the Arsenal keeper to make it 5-3. The crowd were being treated to a magnificent spectacle from both teams and, even with only a few minutes remaining, the tempo of the game didn't let up at all. Arsenal pulled one back with just over ten minutes to go. Roger Byrne had received a nasty knock to his thigh, but carried on, shoring up his defence until the final whistle eventually came. It was, and would remain, one of the most famous ever victories for United. Acknowledging that they had just taken part in a vintage game, the players sportingly congratulated each other and the home crowd cheered both teams as they left the field.

Exhausted from the game, but exhilarated as well, United now looked forward to the game against Red Star. At the same time, the players were full of trepidation about the prospect of going to another communist country. For those who had been to Prague, the depressing atmosphere of life in a communist state had not been particularly enjoyable. For some other of the players it was the first time. In 1958, little was known about life in a Soviet country. Was it safe? What would their reception be like? How would Red Star play? Within just a few days, they would find out the answers to all their questions.

5

BELGRADE

On the Monday morning after the exhausting, exhilarating game at Highbury, the team congregated at Old Trafford to fly out to Belgrade. That morning also happened to be the Fifth Round draw of the FA Cup and some of the players had come early to listen to the draw live on the radio. Those who had already arrived went down to the laundry rooms, where there was a radio. The laundry room was run by two ladies, Irene Ramsden and her sister, Mrs Taylor, who were known as Omo and Daz, after two well-known soap powders. They were responsible for washing all the club kits, but some of the players brought their own washing in, too. In order to dry the huge numbers of shirts and shorts, the ladies used to hang the washing on a long line between the stadium and the railway that runs alongside Old Trafford. In the Fifth Round, United were drawn at home against Sheffield Wednesday. A tough match, but a home draw, at least.

Eventually, all the players had arrived, all except one, that is. "The morning we were going to Belgrade," says Harry Gregg, "Mark [Jones] was late and he come bounding over about half an hour late and he wore this little trilby. This guy was huge, he was a huge man. Only in his twenties, but massive, blond hair, big round face, big round head. And as he gets in the boss says to him, 'You're a bit late big fellow'. And d'you know what it was? He bred budgies and one of 'em had took ill during the night and he sat up with it all night and he fell asleep and that's why he was late." Jones loved his birds so much that he had been perfectly prepared to miss the match because of them. "You should have gone without me," Jones complained.

With all the players finally assembled, they climbed aboard their coach and left for Ringway airport. Jimmy Murphy saw them off, saying "See you Thursday, lads."

Murphy had been due to accompany the team, as he always did, but as the result of an extraordinary series of events, he was needed elsewhere.

In their World Cup qualifying table, Wales had finished runners up and so had missed out on qualifying for the 1958 World Cup Finals. In another qualifying group, there were only two teams – Israel and Turkey, but Turkey refused to play the Israelis and FIFA had no choice but to disqualify Turkey and let Israel through to the next stage, a play-off with the qualifying team from Asia. This was Indonesia, who wanted to play their game against Israel on neutral ground, but FIFA refused and so Indonesia withdrew. Israel's next opponents, Sudan, who were only through because Egypt had earlier withdrawn, also refused to play against Israel and so Israel went through to the Finals without having played a single game!

In those days, this bizarre set of events was not uncommon, the tournament apparently being run as a lottery rather than as a credible football competition. Before the qualifying rounds even began, for instance, FIFA had rejected the entries of Kenya and Korea into the competition without any explanation. During qualification, Venezuela inexplicably withdrew from the competition, as did Cyprus and China, and the game between Curaçao and Guatemala was not played because the Guatemalan players were not permitted to travel to Curaçao.

As a result of these kinds of quirks and flukes, FIFA ruled that every team that had made it through the qualifiers to the World Cup Finals should have played at least one competitive game. In order to find replacement opposition for Israel, FIFA put the names of all the group runners up into a hat and picked one. The team they picked was Belgium, who declined to play. The next team out of the hat was Wales, who agreed.

This special play-off would take place over two legs. Wales won 2-0 in the away game and the home leg was to be played at Ninian Park the same day that United were playing Red Star. Murphy had agonised over which game to attend, but Busby decided for him. He told Murphy that his role as Manager of Wales must take priority over his responsibilities at Manchester United. In the event, Wales won 2-0 and so they, as well as England, Scotland and Northern Ireland, were off to Sweden in the summer. It was the first and only time that all four home nations attended the World Cup Finals on the same occasion.

In Murphy's place, Busby took Bert Whalley along. He and Tom Curry would look after the boys before and after the match and would be a reassuring presence throughout the whole trip. Also on the plane for the Belgrade trip was a press corps made up of nine of the best sports writers in the north of England: Alf Clarke of the *Manchester Evening Chronicle*; Don Davies of the *Manchester Guardian*; George Follows of the *Daily Herald*; Tom Jackson of the *Manchester Evening News*; Archie Ledbrooke of the *Daily Mirror*; Henry Rose of the *Daily Express*; Frank Swift of the *News of the World*; Frank Taylor of the *News Chronicle* and Eric Thompson of the *Daily Mail*. Busby and the players knew these journalists very well. The writers would often hang around in the bowels of the grounds on a Saturday afternoon and fraternise with the players after the game. In addition to weekend games, these writers also travelled with the players to midweek games in Europe. They flew together, stayed in the same hotels, ate and drank with the players and held post-match analyses with them. Ever since United's entry into European competition, public interest was so huge that newspapers could justify the cost of sending their writers out.

When Frank Swift had initially asked the *News of the World* to send him to Yugoslavia to report on United's game against Red Star Belgrade, however, the paper turned him down. The World Cup qualifying play-off between Wales and Israel was deemed much more important for the paper to cover. Busby got wind of this and stepped in, offering Swift a free seat on the club's privately chartered aircraft. Perhaps Busby was mindful of the fact that United needed, and benefited from, as much media coverage as possible. On the other hand, there were already eight other journalists travelling with the team and so maybe Busby was just doing Swift a favour. In any case, Swift accepted.

Busby and Swift were great friends and had been ever since their playing days together at Manchester City, where Busby had kept an eye on the young goalkeeper. During the war, they played in the same army team and when England beat Scotland at Hampden Park in 1945, it was Swift who saved Busby's penalty. They had been great colleagues and rivals and now they were great friends. Swift lived on the King's Road, just round the corner from Busby, and the two bumped into each other all the time.

At Ringway, the party began boarding flight 609 to Belgrade via Munich. For this special trip abroad, Walter Crickmer had hired a particularly luxurious aircraft – a BEA Airspeed Ambassador, 'Elizabethan' class. The interior of the Elizabethan was much more lavish than the Viscounts and

Dakotas the players were used to. The cabin was much larger, with a central aisle and ten rows of two very plush seats either side. The aircraft was particularly unusual in that the first six rows from the back of the plane were forward-facing and the remaining four rows at the front faced the rear of the plane. On the port side, where the forward-facing and rear-facing seats met was another unusual feature – a one-off group of six seats, perfect for a game of cards. Harry Gregg was a big poker player and he had quickly joined the card-school that played on all these away games and which had Ray Wood, Johnny Berry, Roger Byrne, Jackie Blanchflower and Billy Whelan as members.

Once the players were safely strapped in, the plane took off without incident and landed at Munich to refuel a couple of hours later – the Elizabethan's fuel tanks were not large enough for a non-stop flight. The descent into Belgrade airport was made slightly more difficult than usual because of low cloud and fog. But Captain Rayment, who was very experienced with Elizabethan aircraft and who had piloted the flight that took United to Bilbao the year before, brought the plane down safely and skilfully, so much so, in fact, that the airport engineers didn't realise the plane had landed at all until it taxied into its bay.

The team disembarked and were driven to their hotel. It was dark by this time, so the players couldn't see much in the gloom. When they got to their hotel, The Majestic, it was, in Gregg's words, "magnificent". Tall, modern and glass-fronted, it was an impressive building run by the State exclusively for visiting foreigners. Grand staircases rose either side of the main entrance and a huge lift system lay ahead of them. The central heating pumped out heat to almost unbearable levels. There was a dining area at the rear of the hotel, and a patio overlooking the river Danube, sluggish and murky rather than blue.

Apart from injury, the thing most likely to prevent a player from playing whilst abroad was illness through food. It was Tom Curry and Bert Whalley's job to make sure that the food served to the players was as close to English food as possible – they couldn't run the risk of the players eating anything too seasoned or spicy. As was the case in Czechoslovakia, Tom Curry had asked the players to bring food with them, which they did by the suitcase-full: ham, Spam, corned beef, bacon, hardboiled eggs, soup, sugar, beans, biscuits, chocolate and fruit. Walter Crickmer was also a cook, and his job was to put together a main meal every evening for the players if the food in Belgrade turned out to be too 'foreign'. Ever attentive, however, the hotel kitchen staff made sure to cook meals that were as similar to English food as they could possibly get, and all the meals they were served during their stay in the hotel were first-rate. In the end, none of the food they had brought with them was needed and the players gave it all away to the hotel staff. Bobby Charlton gave his four packs of biscuits to a somewhat bemused cleaner.

Staying in the hotel for the first evening, Busby and the players gathered in the hotel bar. Eddie Colman and Bill Whelan entertained the rest of the players with their famous impersonation of the South American rumba. Upstairs, Tom Curry was treating the doubtful Roger Byrne. His thigh, so badly bruised at Highbury, had still not healed and Curry applied an old-fashioned poultice. Tired after their long journey, everyone turned in early.

The following morning, United went for a light training session at a pitch next to Red Star's ground. The pitch was in an awful state – where it wasn't waterlogged, it was icy and the whole thing was a quagmire. Unperturbed, the team ran out and did some jogging, watched by both the English and Yugoslav press, the captains and cabin crew of the aircraft and 200 or so assorted Yugoslavs. Whilst doing laps around the pitch, Edwards picked up a young Yugoslav boy and hauled him onto his back, carrying him round for half a lap. They then kicked a ball around the mud for an hour or so. Roger Byrne tested his thigh and gave the thumbs up – he was fit enough for the game the next day. Geoff Bent wouldn't be needed after all.

In the darkness that evening, they were allowed out to have a 'proper' look around the city for the first time. They went out in groups of twos and threes, but were always accompanied by armed guards and interpreters and were never allowed to wander too far. Albert Scanlon remembers the streets being well-lit and the main shops being full of goods, and remembers that people moved out of their way when they walked around. Despite the heavy chaperone, however, the players didn't have to look too hard to see that life was very tough in Yugoslavia. Off the main drag, the housing was uniformly drab and badly maintained and there were numerous food queues. Signs of deprivation were all around. Harry Gregg remembers that he "actually saw people with vehicle tyres, motorbike tyres or something, laced with cord on their feet for shoes."

The authorities did their best to present the best possible face of Tito's Communist system. During the course of their stay, the players were not only served first-class food, but they were taken out to shows and films, always accompanied by armed guards and a fleet of interpreters. But, although the friendliness shown to the players by the people they came across and the hospitality shown to them by their hosts was second to none, it sat uneasily with the obvious hardship around them.

After another light training session on the Wednesday morning, the players finally arrived at Partisans Stadium for the big game. As the team made their way through the large crowd that had gathered to welcome them, the locals chanted "Red Devils! Red Devils!". The people of Belgrade

were clearly delighted to have United in their city. Red
Star Belgrade had been relatively unknown to the English
public before the fixture against Manchester United, but
the people in Yugoslavia knew all about Matt Busby's team.
Tommy Taylor, Duncan Edwards *et al* were stars, and heroes.
In a newspaper interview before this game, Sekularac himself
had acknowledged what a great side United were. Asked
for his prediction on the result, Sekularac said, amazingly,
"Manchester too strong. Manchester will win."

The pitch in the stadium itself was in much better shape
than the practice pitch. It had been covered in snow the day
before the match, but the sun had come out that day, leaving
only patches of snow here and there. The game had provoked
an unprecedented scramble for tickets and was a complete
sell-out. Any niceties previously shown to the United players
vanished once the players emerged from their dressing room.
The arena they entered that afternoon at 3 o'clock was one
of the most intimidating they ever had to play in. The crowd
began viciously whistling at the United players and a mass
shout went up of "Plavi! Plavi!" ("Up the blues!"). Hundreds
of Yugoslav Army soldiers dressed in khaki uniforms had been
deployed around the ground to separate the heckling crowd
from the players. Bill Foulkes described the atmosphere inside
the ground as "unbelievable" and Harry Gregg said that he
never played another game in front of such a hostile crowd.

It was Manchester United, though, who got off to a flying
start. Within two minutes of the whistle blowing they were
one up, courtesy of a goal from Dennis Viollet. As he often
did, Tommy Taylor had picked up the ball on the half way
line after it had been cleared from United's defence. He took
it into the box, running past two or three Red Star players in
the process and, instead of shooting, unselfishly passed it to
Viollet. Wearing his trademark black shirt, Beara came out of
goal, but Viollet easily slotted it past him. The goal stunned the

52,000 crowd into silence. Red Star supporters had thought they could comfortably overhaul the 2-1 deficit from the first leg, but 3-1 looked much tougher.

After the restart, Red Star's Sekularac responded by bringing Duncan Edwards down and damaging his ankle, perhaps in retaliation for Edwards' shoulder charge in the first leg. Seemingly blind to what was clearly a foul, the referee waved play on. A few moments later, Charlton scored from Scanlon's fantastically placed corner kick, but the referee whistled for offside. He was pointing to Scanlon, who was still out by the corner flag and obviously not participating in the game. The United team sensed that, for whatever reason, the Austrian referee, Karl Kainer, was giving decisions Belgrade's way. The crowd started up their noisy support for Red Star again, even resorting to throwing snowballs at the United players every time they came near the Red Star goal. Despite this and the decisions going against them, however, United dominated the first half with their possession play and beautiful attacking football. Half an hour into the first half, Charlton finished off a typically fluent passing move and slotted the ball home. A few minutes later, Charlton scored again. Beara, the Belgrade keeper, had boasted before the game that no one had ever beaten him with a shot from outside the penalty area, but Bobby Charlton did just that, a belter from 25 yards that quietened the crowd and silenced Red Star altogether. For the rest of the first half, Eddie Colman was particularly instrumental in many more attacks, but United failed to stretch their lead any further. Nevertheless, at the half-time whistle, United went back to the dressing room an inconceivable 5-1 up on aggregate.

As was often the case with United, however, their second half wasn't a patch on their first. Red Star started off brightly and, just after half time, Kostic, their inside-left, floated a shot from outside the box that beat the helpless Gregg. From then on, their tails up, Red Star started to play the better attacking football and United didn't seem to have an answer. Matters weren't helped by the fact that Red Star's dangerous tackles still went unpunished. The worst culprit was again Sekularac, who ran his studs down Ken Morgans' thigh, leaving a nasty open wound. He got away with only a warning from the referee. Morgans limped off the field. Ten minutes after Red Star's first goal, Tasic slipped and fell inside United's penalty area and dragged Bill Foulkes down with him. To the utter disbelief of the United players, the referee awarded Red Star a penalty, which Tasic duly converted. Suddenly, at 3-2 on the night and 5-3 on aggregate, Red Star now had all the momentum.

Helped on by the whistles and jeers from the crowd, they came at United again and again. United's defence held out but, every time United made what they considered a fair tackle, the referee awarded a free kick. By the end of the game, the referee had awarded 24 free kicks against United as opposed to just 11 against Red Star. "We stopped tackling because good tackles were being punished with free kicks," Roger Byrne said after the game. To make up numbers, Kenny Morgans hobbled back onto the field after having been revived with some whisky.

Red Star continued to put United under tremendous pressure. Harry Gregg came out and dived to smother yet another challenge and, though he collected the ball, he also slid outside the penalty area – a free kick to Red Star. Because Gregg's white shorts had red all over them, Roger Byrne thought Gregg was badly injured in the challenge. In order to make out the pitch in the snow, the lines had been painted in red, not the usual white, and it was only this dye that Byrne saw. With just a few minutes left, Red Star's expert at set pieces, Kostic, stepped up and curled the ball round the wall. The shot deflected off Dennis Viollet's head and Gregg could only palm the ball into the back of the net. Scanlon says that it was the first time he ever saw a football curled round a wall. Behind Gregg's goal, the crowd surged forwards, pushing against a low brick wall which collapsed under the pressure, allowing the crowd to spill out onto the grass. They were only kept off the pitch by a line of Yugoslav Army soldiers. The crowd were pressing so hard that Gregg was pushed in the back by the soldiers. United restarted and Red Star attacked again. Scanlon frantically cleared the ball, kicking it up field and chasing after it. In the last minute of the game, Scanlon took the ball into Red Star's area and chipped Beara. The ball hit the post and rebounded towards Tommy Taylor, but his shot went wide. At that very moment, the referee at last blew for the end of the game. United had done it: 3-3 on the night but 5-4 on aggregate.

Never before were they so relieved to hear the final whistle. The players hugged each other, realising their achievement, but they were also absolutely exhausted. Harry Gregg explains: "You can't describe what you feel. For a split second, for a short period you're full of it, but then after that it appears to be an anticlimax. You're full of it, but everything's drained out of you because it's not just the physical side, it's the mental side when you play this game, especially if you play at the highest level. There's a lot of pent- up emotion in it, but there's always a flatness afterwards." Busby declared it their best ever performance in Europe while Red Star's keeper, Beara, had to admit grudgingly after the game that "Manchester United are the better qualified team for the semi-final."

When the team coach left the stadium, it was booed by the crowd all the way back to the hotel, but United's reception at the Majestic was altogether different. Dressed in their club blazers and ties, the players were shown into a banqueting hall where a sumptuous meal was laid on for both teams. Once seated, violinists played discreetly in the background, while a fleet of waiters served the dishes on candle-lit, ice-laden trays.

The lavishness of the evening greatly impressed the United party, but one thing in particular features in all the players' memories of the evening.

At the time, the Soviet Union was in the middle of its Sputnik space programme and in the banqueting hall that night was an imitation Sputnik space rocket, three feet long with a tail, moving round the banqueting hall on a rail suspended from the ceiling. The Sputnik kept circling the huge room all night, throughout dinner and even the after- dinner speeches. It was a source of great amusement for all the United party.

Although the Yugoslav players were, obviously, disappointed to be knocked out of the European Cup, the two teams got on well that evening. Sekularac sat next to Bobby Charlton, who soon nicknamed him 'Shecky'. There was a great deal of mutual respect between the two men and a friendship was forged that night that would last for many years. There was plenty of wine and beer and, after the banquet was over, each of the players was given a set of coffee cups as a commemorative gift. When all the pomp and ceremony was finally over, the players started singing, as they always did. Usually, Jimmy Murphy would accompany them on a piano, but this time it was *a cappella*. Roger Byrne led the singing of *We'll Meet Again*, but the highlight of the evening was Matt Busby's rendition of *I Belong to Glasgow*. The players joined in the chorus, but only Busby knew the words to all the verses.

Harry Gregg takes up the story: "I'll never forget the night of the banquet and the players had been told, according to how things went, they could go out and enjoy themselves, which was Matt's way, by the way, wonderful like that. And it got to about twelve o'clock and everybody was singing and the sputnik was going round the ceiling and then big Mark Jones started singing, *On Ilkley Moor Baht 'at*, and I mean broad Yorkshireman. David Pegg from Doncaster, Tommy Taylor from Barnsley and big Mark Jones and there's the three of

them, with a few beers in them, singing *On Ilkley Moor Baht
'at*. Wonderful. Roger Byrne sitting about two seats from me
is writing on a napkin. I thought, what the hell's he at? And
I watched the napkin be passed up the length of our table,
along the top table to the boss who was smoking his pipe, I
watched him open the napkin and nod his head and I said,
'What was that all about?' Roger said 'He promised us we
could go out'. Roger wanted to know is it still okay because
time had gone on, it was late heading into the early hours
of the morning, half past twelve. Broke up, a fair number
went back to the hotel, which was grand, quite a few more
headed to the British Embassy, including I think the pilot. We
went back to the hotel and into a room to play poker. And
remember, I was not as versed in travel as a lot of these smart
arses I was playing with. I was a big green lad from Doncaster
Rovers and gone there as a star, but these guys had travelled
before this star and travelled further. We played cards and I
had a great night, I was winning everything. But during the
night – I'm talking two and three and four in the morning
– somebody said, 'Let's open our suitcases' and one or two
in the room opened their suitcases and there we were eating
hardboiled eggs – we didn't need to, they would have gone
rotten anyway. Maybe corned beef, opened a tin of corned
beef. That was it in the middle of the night, lads enjoying
themselves. Well I had a very good night in the card school. We
then broke up, headed to our rooms – it wasn't worth going
to bed – headed to our room – it was a grand hotel – shoes
outside the door for them to be polished and so forth. Now
they said Henry [Rose] didn't take drink. Well all I know is,
around four o'clock in the morning as I come out of the card
school, Henry was trying to get into his bedroom, he must
have returned from a club or embassy and he couldn't find the
keyhole, and I said, 'Can I help you?' because to me he was a
hero you see, this was a top press man as all of them were, all

those press men were and they should be remembered. And I said, 'Henry, can I help you?' because Henry was trying to open the door with the key on the side that the hinges were on and the lock doesn't go there. And he said, 'Thank you very much' and headed into his room. Little Eddie Colman appeared on the scene and he was his usual self, lovely Jack the Lad, little tubby lad, and he was moving shoes, mixing shoes up at doors till somebody said, 'Hey Coley, that's the boss's shoes'. You never seen shoes go back so quick to where they belonged."

Dennis Viollet, the most inveterate nightclub-goer amongst the players, wanted to sample Belgrade's nightlife, but was told that there weren't many places to go and, besides, they were all shut. He and Frank Swift ended up going down to the hotel bar and sat up all night talking about the game. Bill Foulkes and Albert Scanlon, along with the pilots, stewardesses and the radio operator, were taken for drinks at the British Embassy staff club. Afterwards, they were invited by some of the Embassy staff to their homes for a nightcap. Foulkes and Scanlon were given a bottle of gin each before they headed back to the hotel. Roger Byrne, Duncan Edwards and Tommy Taylor, on the other hand, had been taken by a Yugoslav sports reporter called Miro Radojcic to a club called The Crystal Bar, which was one of the very few nightspots in Belgrade. It was nearly dawn when the three of them returned to their hotel to snatch a few hours' sleep before leaving for the airport.

Radojcic, however, stayed on at the club, reflecting on the conversation he'd had with the young United players. He had been impressed with their professionalism and playing ability and was thinking about the feature he was due to write the next morning for a sports journal called *Politika*. He decided to ask if he could fly to England with them to write an article about the brilliant young team from their point of view. It would be a scoop for him. Returning to his apartment, Radjocic packed a small bag, then caught a taxi straight to the airport. In exchange for a long and detailed article, he felt sure the club would allow him to fly with them back to Manchester.

THE CRASH

The following morning – Thursday 6th February – was crisp, cold and clear. The sky was blue and there was a smattering of snow on the ground. The heads of the United players, however, were far from clear. Most had had just a few hours' sleep. Leaving the hotel in their team coach very early, they disembarked at Belgrade airport and hung around, waiting in the cold until they could board their plane and go back to sleep. Miro Radojcic was already at the airport, waiting for the coach's arrival and, when he asked if he, too, could join the party, he was told that he was more than welcome. His gamble had paid off.

At a time when flying in Europe, especially from behind the Iron Curtain, was far less common than it is today, the United party had a few extra travellers that morning other than Radojcic, all of whom wanted to take advantage of the rare flight to England. Also joining them that morning was the Yugoslav travel agent who had organised the trip, Mr Miklos, and his wife, Eleanor; Mrs Vera Lukic, the wife of the Yugoslav air attaché in London, and her 22-month old baby daughter;

and Mr Tomasevic, a Yugoslav journalist. Boarding began, and it was then that Radojcic discovered, much to his annoyance, that he had left his passport at home. He asked the officials to delay take-off for as long as possible and hurriedly found a taxi to take him back to his apartment.

The others boarded the Elizabethan plane from the rear. Inside the plush, spacious cabin, the United card school made straight for the six-seater. Harry Gregg had cleaned them out of all their dinars the night before and they wanted their revenge. Byrne, Berry, Whelan, Jackie Blanchflower and Ray Wood pointed to a seat for Gregg, but Gregg wanted to let them sweat a bit longer. He declined their invitation, saying that he was tired and lay down on a two-seater across the aisle from them.

The plane took off without incident and the players and pressmen did what they usually do to kill time on flights like this: sleep, play cards, read, do crosswords, talk or just look out the window at the snowy peaks 18,000 feet below. Dennis Viollet and Bobby Charlton were chatting to Eddie Colman in the back of the plane. Harry Gregg was fast asleep. All the reporters, bar Frank Taylor, were sitting at the back. They, too, had a card school going, one that had started on Monday when they got on the plane, carried on in the hotel and after the banquet, and now on the return journey home. There was no time to serve breakfast for the whole party during the short flight – the hungry passengers had been promised a meal when the plane was airborne for Manchester.

As the plane approached Munich, the cloud cover became very dense. The plane lurched horribly on its descent into Reim airport, causing everyone's stomach to leap into their mouths. No one could see anything out the window because of the low-lying cloud; it was only at the last minute that fields and buildings could be seen rushing by. It was snowing heavily, but Thain and Rayment managed to bring the plane safely down onto the runway, slush spraying out in huge waves from the wheels. The brakes went on and the plane gradually slowed and began its taxi to the terminal building. The players had been told that their stopover in Munich was only going to be brief, so once inside, some wandered off visiting shops to buy souvenirs, while others sat in the coffee lounge, smoking and drinking coffee. As there were no airport staff to hand, Eleanor Miklos, who was born in England, took it upon herself to serve the coffee.

In the meantime, Captains Thain and Rayment were completing their flight plan in the Met office. In such atrocious weather conditions, the main worry was snow collecting on the wings. This would make the plane considerably heavier and therefore interfere with lift-off. Thain had carefully watched the snow falling on the wings. It thawed as soon as it hit the metal and Thain could see water running off the trailing edge – there was no need to apply any de-icer to the wings and they didn't need to be swept. There were only two minor things to be done to the aircraft before take-off: the pump in one of the toilets had broken and the cold water tank for the galley needed refilling. Once the tank was filled, Thain ordered the passengers back on the plane.

At 14:30, the Elizabethan had been fully inspected, fully refuelled and was ready for take-off. After taxiing back out, her engines were opened up at the head of the runway and, once at full power, she began to gather speed for take-off. As she progressed down the runway, she slipped a little in the snow. Frank Taylor was looking out one of the fore port windows, watching to see the aircraft leave the ground and the port wheel retract. All he could see was a wave of slush thrown clear, like the wave of water from the bow of a boat. The plane continued at speed down the runway, bobbing up and down and skidding in the snow when, suddenly, there was a huge judder and the plane braked, dramatically losing speed. Looking very alarmed, the cabin steward, Tom Cable, ran into a spare seat and strapped himself in. The aircraft drew to a grinding halt half way down the runway. Captain Thain noticed there had been a wild surge in boost pressure and reasoned it was this that had most probably caused to the plane to shudder. He and Rayment checked their gauges and dials – temperature and pressure were ok, the warning lights were out – and requested permission for another attempt, which the Control Tower granted.

Taxiing back to the head of the runway, the Elizabethan was soon ready to try again. It was 14:35. The throttles were opened to full power and she gathered speed down the runway a second time. A minute later, as her speed was building, exactly the same thing happened – a horrible shuddering of the plane and a sudden, dramatic loss of speed. Once again, the needle on the dial indicated that there had been an alarming boost in pressure. Something was clearly not right, so Captain Thain told the passengers over the intercom that there was a "slight engine fault" and that they would be returning to find out what the matter was.

Back in the airport lounge, the players sat down for what they thought might be a long wait. Some wandered around the shops, others were once again served coffee by Eleanor Miklos. Harry Gregg gave a cigarette to Jackie Blanchflower and was just about to light it for him when the passengers were called to the aircraft again. Everyone was very surprised as they had only just disembarked and had been in the lounge only a few minutes. Even so, thinking that everything must be all right and encouraged to be on their way again so quickly, they collected their belongings and headed across the snowy tarmac to the waiting plane.

Whilst the players were in the lounge, Captain Thain had informed the airport engineer of the wild surges in boost pressure. The engineer said that it wasn't an uncommon occurrence at an airport as high up as Munich. Thain had never flown into Munich in an Elizabethan before, but Rayment had and he confirmed what the engineer said. The two Captains looked at the wings – they were in perfectly good shape and did not need sweeping at all. Fuel tanks were full, all instrumentation was normal: there seemed no good reason not to try for take-off a third time and so the call was made for the passengers to board the aircraft. It was 2:45pm.

Harry Gregg takes up the story: "When I climbed on board the aircraft on the third attempt, you know the steward sees you on board, as I climbed in – and to this day I feel terrible – I climbed up the steps, turned left and strapped in the back seat was Tom Cable the steward, poor fellow, strapped petrified, because of what happened on the first attempt. And instead of seeing us on board, that poor fellow was strapped in the back seat of the aircraft. Made my way in, we started to go and I looked diagonally across at Roger Byrne and I didn't know Roger was a bad flyer and his face was contorted and my, me as a human being, thought he's more worried than I am and I sort of laughed out of that, you know, like you get courage from somebody else's weakness. And that little Johnny Berry was sitting between him and Liam Whelan said, 'We're all gonna get friggin' killed here'. That's true. And Liam Whelan just said quietly, 'Well if it happens, I'm ready'. That was it. We went, I looked at Bill Foulkes in front of me, Bill would not be as tall as I am and I could see the top of his head over the seat and above him, above our heads was the bulkhead where the whole plane comes together. In my silly Irish way I thought, if this thing bellyflops – I swear that's all I thought – if it bellyflops he'll jab his brains in. So what I did, with me being taller, I got down lower in my seat and made sure my seat was above my head. I opened the front of my trousers because we are all afraid of the soft part of our body, that is fact. I opened the front of my trousers, even my

waistband, I put my feet up on Foulkesy's chair, I opened my
tie and pulled it down to there. And off we went and kept
watching out the window. I watched the snow, I watched the
bow wave and I kept watching houses and I thought, we've
made it, and I watched the wheels come up, and that was it.
Just darkness and daylight and sparks and sparks and sparks
and darkness, complete darkness. As the whole thing broke
up, I can honestly say, I just thought…I won't see my wife
and my little girl again, I won't see my mum and I can't speak
German, that's all I thought. And I thought, you can't describe
it as slowly as I thought it. And then all of a sudden it was just
complete darkness. I felt the top of my head and I felt the
blood coming down, I was afraid to put my hand up, I thought
the top of my head had been taken off like a hardboiled egg,
and I felt the blood run down my face and I just lay there in
the darkness and I couldn't figure, it was daylight, why was it
dark. And the blood ran, I reached down to unfasten my safety
belt and didn't realise that I didn't have a safety belt, I was
half buried, where the plane had tilted slightly on one side
and my side was, the window was, the window I talked about
was half under the ground. And a way up, after a few seconds
– there was no screaming, there was no shouting and there
was no crying, there was just a terrible, terrible, tearing of
metal, sparks, darkness, daylight, like opening up and closing
up. There was no crying, there wasn't a cry, there wasn't a
squeal or a shout, there was nothing but horrendous tearing
and blackness, not what all the cowboys tell you, it's not true.
And I just lay there and I looked up and to my right and
above me there was a shaft of light and I reached down, as I
said before, and I started to crawl and I was crawling up an
incline. And I got to the hole, I put my head through the hole,
it wasn't big enough for me to get out, and lying below me
on the ground was the youth team, Bert Whalley that had
developed all the young players, and he'd been taken there as

a bonus, and he was lying on the ground in an air force grey
suit and his eye was wide open, he had one eye, a glass eye
'cos he lost his eye with playing football, and there wasn't a
mark on him. And I turned myself round, on my backside,
and I kicked the hole bigger and I dropped down on the
ground beside Bert Whalley and for a split second I didn't
know what was going on. I thought, I'm the only one alive
here, I don't even know what I thought. And in the distance
I could see five people running and one of them turned and
shouted, a fair way away, 'Run, run, run'. And just with that
round what was left of the cockpit – and I'll show it to you,
you'll not believe it – came a very brave man, the captain, Jim
Thain, and he shouted – he had a fire extinguisher in his hand
– 'Run you stupid bastard, it's going to explode' in his pukka
English. And he turned and went back the way he came and
I heard a child crying... I heard the child, and I shouted,
'Come back, there's people alive in here'. And at that stage in
my life for me to swear off a football pitch was like missing
Mass or something, or not going to confessions, but I was so
angry I shouted, 'Come back you bastards, there's people alive
in here', that was anger, or fear. I made my way back in through
the hole again and I was terrified of what I'd find. I was
honestly terrified, I didn't want to find anything. And
eventually I found what they called in those days a romper
suit, a little bunny suit and there was nothing in it, in the
darkness. And I crawled a bit further and eventually I found
a baby. I crawled out, I started to run when I got down on
the ground, shouting, and they saw me and a fellow called
Rogers, the radio operator, he came running back and I said,
'There's people alive' and I handed him the child and he took
the child off me and ran back to our people again and the
people concerned were, Ted Ellyard, telegraphist for *The Daily
Mail*, Peter Howard the photographer, the two stewardesses
and Rogers, the operator, those were the five people. And I

went back in again and eventually I found the lady, or let's
say she found me, the thing exploded in the darkness, exploded
her in the wreckage and she was incredible. Her face was
completely flat like a wall, flat as my hand, it was as pure black
as that there, I got her to the hole, I didn't get her out, I got
her to the hole, I put my two feet in the middle of her back
and kicked her out through the hole and she kept going. That
woman was smashed in pieces, legs and everything and kept
going. And I didn't carry her, I kicked her out. I then went
back and I found Joe Friday [Albert Scanlon]. I found Ray
Wood and Joe Friday, Albert with his head cracked in two
places, from there – the mark's still there yet – into there, you
see through his hair, and from there into there, just like you
overboil an egg, it was cracked open…. That's how Albert was.
He was trapped, the blood was coming out of his ears and
everything. I tried to pull him out, I couldn't get him out, he
was trapped by the legs. I had to drop him. I then found Ray
Wood, I can tell you what Ray Wood was wearing – that's
red – he was wearing an orange pullover, we talked about it
since, he says, 'Christ Greggy, you have some memory'. He
was wearing an orange pullover, a v-necked pullover and I
tried to get Woody out and he'd damaged one of his eyes, he
was trapped as well and I will tell you exactly what I thought.
Oh poor old Woody, he won't bother me again. 'Cos he was
the other goalkeeper. Now that sounds a terrible thing, but
that's true. I came out through the hole, I started shouting,
shouting, 'Blanchy, Blanchy, Blanchy' and you know the
connection. He was the one guy that I really knew, we'd been
at school and played for our country together. And I called
Blanchy and Blanchy and I went round what was left, Bert
Whalley's lying here, the stump of an engine there, that was
the plane, was completely ripped off. I went round there and
found lying half in and half out of the damn thing, was Dennis
Viollet and Bobby Charlton. Dennis Viollet had a terrible,

terrible cut behind his ear. Bobby Charlton was basically unmarked. I took them for dead, I grabbed them in the snow by the waistband of their trousers – and I was a big strong fellow – and pulled them as far away as I could, fifteen yards or something, and left them for dead. I then came round to the other side and that's when I saw a house with the roof off it and the roof burning, and further up I seen a huge explosion and the rest of the aeroplane, the nose on it, were in there. Let them all tell you the romantic tale they want to. I moved round there between the burning compound, the rest of the aeroplane, all of the aeroplane, and the house there with half the roof off it and there lying in the snow, as I'm sitting here, but on his elbows was the manager. And I stopped with him and he had a slight, slight – he's bald – slight cut behind his ear, it was nothing. Compared to what I'd seen before I got there and he kept just moaning and moaning, rubbing his chest and saying, 'Oh my leg, my leg, my leg. Oh my legs'. But compared to what I'd seen he was okay. So I got a lot of rubbish that was lying – it's hard to believe what was lying about – and jammed it under his back and just kept saying, 'You're okay boss, you're okay' and jammed it under his back and went looking for others, made him comfortable. And about fifteen yards from them I found Jackie, and Jackie was crying and he was lying in the snow and Roger Byrne – Jack was lying flat out in the snow and Roger was lying across his waist and Roger did not have a mark on him and his eyes – handsome man – his eyes were open, he didn't have a mark on him. Whether he'd done the same as me or not I don't know, but it stuck with me for years, his white Y-fronts, his trousers were open. Whether he'd done the same as I'd done or they'd been blown open and for a long time I used to think, why didn't I close his eyes. I was only a young fellow myself. And Jackie was crying, 'I've broke my back, I've broke my back'. And I said, 'You're okay Blanchy', I looked down and his right arm was hanging off. And I didn't say to him and I was just mumbling, 'Blanchy you're okay, you're okay' and he's crying and the snow's melting because there's a fire, I can see it now. And I took my tie off, I took my tie off and I tied it round the stump of his arm and I broke it. And I'm scrabbling about in the snow and mud and stuff looking for something to tie his arm with and I sensed, and I looked up, and one of the poor girls, the stewardesses, that's the first person I seen, she was looking down at me and her eyes were that size, I'm not using the Irish tales, her eyes were like organ stops. And I said, 'Love, for Christ's sake get me something to tie his arm with. Get me something to tie his arm with'. And she just stared and stared and stared, the poor girl. And I used half of my tie and tied Jackie's arm up. And by that time, ordinary – I repeat, ordinary – German people came across the fields from a railway track and eventually a man in a Volkswagen van, a blue Volkswagen van and there was people running about and this guy turned up in a tweed coat with a medical bag and he kept running from one to another with a hypodermic syringe and I'm down on my knees with Jackie Blanchflower and I can't speak German and he's running to a body there and I'm shouting, 'He's dead, here' and every time the thing exploded, he ran away. And it sounds funny, till eventually he fell on his arse with a pair of Wellington boots on, a beautiful tweed coat and a hypodermic syringe up in the air. We eventually, the man in the Volkswagen van with a side entry door, a flat van, was helped and we got Matt Busby into it, we got Jackie Blanchflower into it, we got eventually Johnny Berry who I didn't know, I don't know where he came from and he lay in the back of that van, a Volkswagen Caravette van, and I didn't know who he was and I'd played with him, because he had no face and the only reason I knew he was one of us, because he was wearing his blazer. That's fact. I turned round and there was the biggest shock I got, Dennis Viollet and Bobby Charlton just staring at me, and I started to cry. We got them into the van. Bill Foulkes had come from somewhere. The van started to go, Bill Foulkes sat in the front, Dennis Viollet sat beside him and then the driver, it was left-hand drive. And we started to go through the snow and somebody said, 'Stop' and we stopped and we got the body, or the wife of the courier, Mrs Lukic, Mrs Lukic into the van, we stopped and picked her up and she lived and he died. That happens later, and he died at the time. And we headed to where we were going to and the van driver's skidding, going up through the snow and Bill's, poor Bill's nerves had gone and he started punching the man in the back of the neck, I remember Bill punching the head of the driver of the minivan that carried himself and all the bodies from the hospital 'cos we were skidding through the snow and he panicked. Aye. I was become a part of something that, it was only a dream I would become part of it and I realised the dream. Like the story I told you earlier on, Liam Whelan, lovely lad, a very good living Catholic boy and I mean that – lovely lad, quiet lad, very, very great player, had his life taken away tragically. And he's the one that did say on the aeroplane when somebody laughed, little Johnny Berry said, 'What are you laughing about, we could all get fucking killed here'. And Liam Whelan sitting on the outside of the table said, 'Well if it happens I'm ready to go'. And that's not fiction. I don't think he realised it was going to happen, but those were his words.

We got to the hospital, they took us in, we were walking down the corridor and a big huge Yugoslav journalist, Tomasevic – he's died some short time ago – was walking with us, he was on the plane. And all of a sudden he collapsed down the wall, he'd been walking everywhere and his leg was broken in two places and the leg just collapsed in front of us. They carted him away. They took us down to near the front of the hospital and by that time they were bringing bodies in and we were asked, and I was bleeding, and I mean bleeding badly – see, my nose was in two parts and they wanted to stitch it and I said no way, you're not stitching it. So it wasn't only bleeding from being hit, it was bleeding from – you see my nostrils are different, you can see a slight scar there, I wouldn't let them stitch me, I've two different sized… anyway. I eventually was asked to identify people and I identified Ray Wood on the floor while they were operating on him, and we've talked about it since and I said I seen your eye out on your cheek when they were working on it and he said, 'Jesus Christ Greggy, I didn't know that. You're right, I always have trouble with that eye'. I said, 'Woody, I sadly was there and I identified you and watched them with your eye out on your cheek'. And I was the biggest baby of the whole bloody lot. They then took us down, Bobby Charlton – I repeat – Bobby Charlton, Billy Foulkes and myself, that's all, down to a room and they wanted to give us injections, right. And they gave me an injection and put me in a bed, on a trolley and I said, 'I'm not staying in' and I rolled off the trolley. I didn't want to stay in, I just didn't want to, I wanted the hell out of the place. And they gave Foulksy an injection and they wanted to inject Bobby and Bobby was the same even before that, and after, Bobby fainted because he didn't like injections and Bobby Charlton was kept in hospital, that is no story, that's the God's truth, that is the God's truth. So you can add romance to it and heroes and do what you want with it, I don't bloody need it… I'd lost my shoes, lost one shoe and was walking about in my bare, one foot… I went back, I asked could I go to, could I get out, the hell out of it and someone took us, a big, a very, very beautiful blonde German Commandant, as tall as me, a girl, a woman, took us to the Stachus Hotel. And they took us in there, we were taken to the top flat which had what you call – I know I'm a joiner – dormer windows in

it, and I remember standing, in the same room they brought
Peter Howard in and Ted Ellyard. So there was Bill Foulkes,
Peter Howard, Ted Ellyard and myself and I remember looking
out the dormer window as each flake of snow, one at a time,
covered the cars in the streets till they disappeared. That's
how bad the snow eventually got. And being in that room
and taking a drink and the phone rang from reception and
it was the desk to say that the remainder of the crew had
returned to the hotel and were dining in their quarters, in
their suite, would we like to join them and I said yes, I would.
Just anything to keep on the move. We went down. Poor Bill
was still in shock and Captain Thain and I sat and argued
and discussed and he explained to me about flying and he
explained everything about it, told me about the V1, told me
about the V2. I was a carpenter and a professional footballer,
how would I know those things. Told me about drag factor
and told me the reason for the accident. And I lived with that
for up to nearly forty years until that man was proved right
and that man was crucified just the same way as they crucified
Christ, he was not guilty. And the British Government sold
him down the river, rather than upset the German authorities
in Bonn. That is fact. And I always felt for him and that's why I
would speak to his daughter occasionally. What they did to that
man was terrible and it come out in private papers forty years
later. And he explained to me why… I said, 'No, I watched
the undercarriage coming up'. And he told me all about it
and he told me how at the last minute, he told me how they
fly an aeroplane, that the pilots never look out the cockpit. It's
hard to believe. He told me about the left hand, right hand on
the joystick. He told me who the senior captain was, he told
me all that there. I couldn't believe it when he said we watch
the dials. And he told me about the first attempt – who am
I to say – and the dials, the pressure fluctuated. I don't know
those things, a man told me, a professional man. And he said

on the first and second attempt and told me the fluctuation of the dials and then he said, on the third attempt, he said, there's a position in flying an aircraft whether it was V1 and V2. V1 he said you put the anchors on and you've a chance of recovering, he said V2, [which is the] point of no return. You keep going, whether you're going to die or not. At V1 there's a possibility that you might pull up, you can put the brakes on and hope. At V2, you keep going, there's no way out of it. That's what he told me. And he said that they never look through the windows, never look through the thing. He said on the third attempt – and I said, 'I watched the undercarriage coming up Captain, I watched it coming up'. And he told me that at the last split second Ken Rayment lifted his head, looked out the window – and these were his words, 'Christ, we're not gonna make it, lift the undercarriage'. 'Christ, we're not gonna make it, lift the undercarriage'. He looked out of the window, realised he'd come to the end of the runway, never mind the dials, lift the undercarriage, so I'd seen the undercarriage going up as you and I would see flying and think the plane was taking off. That was them lifting it and hoping stopping the whole damn thing. And then she broke up. She hit a house with a woman and two children in it and the lady threw her two children out the window. People never go into that. The two children lived and she lived, she threw her two children out of the window. It took the roof, part of the roof of her house, it carried on, that part of the plane and broke up and the rest [crashed] into a fuel dump, a German fuel dump with a wagon in the compound filled with fuel. And all the rest of the plane, when I first saw it, from the wings to the tail, was completely intact, sticking in this huge fire like a dart. The big German, the beautiful German that brought us [to the Stachus Hotel] – she took a shine to me and I thought that's all I fucking need, I've just got through an air crash. I'm serious too, I'm not being funny. And she was a nice person, I didn't want it and I didn't need it. End of story. And I'm no saint. They took us out and they bought us suits and that was basically it… The following day when I went back there was nothing left. So that's the true story of that anyway. That's that. That is that."

The precise reasons for the crash have never been fully explained. One theory has to do with the position of the undercarriage. It proposes that aircraft with tail-wheel undercarriages were not greatly affected by the build-up of slush, due to the position of these undercarriages in relation to the aircraft's centre of gravity. The Elizabethan, however, had nose-wheel landing-gear, which meant that the main wheels lay behind the centre of gravity, which in turn meant that they were vulnerable to the build-up of slush. The runway at Reim airport is 1,908 metres long but, on the last attempt at take-off that day, the Elizabethan travelled 2,358 metres without ever being able to leave the ground. Obviously, something was very wrong. The term 'V1', which Thain told Gregg about at the dinner table that night, refers to the speed at which it was unsafe to abandon take-off. For the Elizabethan, this speed was 117 knots per hour. The speed needed for lift-off – called V2 – was 119 knots. The problem was that the Elizabethan didn't ever reach V2 that day. In all three attempts at take-off, the engines suddenly lost power at the critical moment and on the third attempt, V1 had been passed and so disaster struck.

The German airport authorities conducted an enquiry into the cause of the crash, during which Captain Thain was question extensively. The enquiry produced two likely reasons: the first was the formation of ice on the wings; the second was that the slush on the runway caused the aircraft to lose speed just at the moment it was due to take off. The enquiry concluded that the former was more likely. The insinuation that Thain was to blame was clear: Captain Thain, who was the same rank as Rayment but who had command of Flight 609, had not detected a build-up of ice and snow on the wings and that this had directly led to the crash.

They defended their conclusion by stating that 16 other aircraft had taken off or landed at Reim airport in complete safety that day, all of which had been de-iced. Thain maintained his position that the wings had been checked for ice and that there had been no need to de-ice the wings. It was later discovered that the German authorities were acting on information about the wings of the Elizabethan gathered a full six hours after the crash, by which time, of course, there was indeed a sheet of ice on the wings.

His name sullied, his reputation tarnished, his position as a professional pilot was deemed no longer tenable and Captain Thain was dismissed by BEA in 1960 but, with BEA's support, he tried to clear his name for many years after the Munich Air Disaster. The German airport authorities maintained their position and conducted two further enquiries, both of which confirmed the original verdict: the blame lay fairly and squarely with Thain for not de-icing the wings. The British, meanwhile, conducted their own enquiry, citing slush on the runway as the probable cause and defending Thain's position. If the cause of the accident had been the slush on the runway, then the blame would lie with the airport authorities; if the cause had been ice on the wings, Thain was liable. Neither side was willing to back down and the legal stalemate dragged on for many years. But, ultimately, the legality lay with the German Federal Government and BEA were eventually forced to settle out of court in 1968 for a sum of £35,000. After the 1968 settlement, Thain had no further resources to carry on his campaign and so gave up. In June 1969, however, in a public statement of support read out in the House of Commons, he was entirely cleared of any blame for the crash.

In 2001, some previously unseen documents declassified by the Foreign Office shed new light on the cause of the Munich Air Disaster. These documents revealed that a German official *had* inspected the Elizabethan aircraft very soon after the crash and had detected no ice on the wings, information that was suppressed at the time by the German government. The documents went on to say that the release of this information by the British government would have led to "a risk of serious damage to our relations with Bonn". All of this was too late for Captain Thain. Much maligned and unfairly accused, Thain was never able to clear his name officially. He never flew again and died of a heart attack in 1975.

Just before his death, exonerated by the British authorities, but still blamed by the Germans, Captain Thain had this to say about the crash: "I don't feel responsible in any way for the crash. Twenty-three people died and it was a terrible tragedy, something that will always be with me. It must be the most publicised air crash of all time, because it involved a famous football team. But if I had died at Munich there is no doubt in my mind that it would have been accepted that the crash had been caused by ice on the wings and the dangers of the slush hazard would not have been realised so soon. How many more people might have lost their lives if I had not been able to battle on?"

As a footnote to the story of the crash: Miro Radojcic never made the flight. In his apartment, he quickly found his passport and returned by taxi to the airport as quickly as possible, but not quickly enough – the flight could not wait for him any longer and had already left. It was the narrowest escape he ever had.

7

THE RECHTS DER ISAR HOSPITAL

A t 3.25pm, twenty minutes after the crash, Professor Georg Maurer, Chief Surgeon at the Rechts der Isar Hospital in Munich, was in the middle of his rounds on the fourth floor of the beautiful old hospital when a nursing orderly called him to the telephone. An official at the airport informed Maurer of the accident and told him the injured were on their way. At that very moment, a fleet of ambulances, their bells ringing, were speeding through the city, following the police cars clearing a way through the traffic. Immediately, Maurer set in motion the hospital's well-drilled emergency procedure.

Short and stout, Maurer was a popular man, an excellent physician and was very well respected by his colleagues. During the war, he had saved the lives of many German and British soldiers on the beaches at Dunkirk, acts of quick thinking in highly stressful situations for which he was awarded the Iron Cross. His wartime experiences had led him to specialise in treating patients who had been involved in accidents like crashes and explosions and, when he was appointed Chief

Surgeon at the Rechts der Isar Hospital, one of the first things
he did was set up a quick-response procedure for victims of
such incidents. The injured people from the Munich Air Crash
could not have been in better hands.

The Volkswagen van carrying Harry Gregg, Bill Foulkes,
Matt Busby, Johnny Berry, Jackie Blanchflower, Dennis Viollet,
Bobby Charlton and Mrs Lukic was the first to arrive outside
the Casualty Department. Those that could walk were led in
through the doors, while the stretcher bearers carried in the
others and laid them down on the ground. Bill Foulkes and
Harry Gregg were given blankets and hot soup and were left
sitting in the corridor as the staff went efficiently about their
business. The ambulances arrived a few minutes later and the
stretchers carrying people both dead and alive began coming
in, soon filling up all the corridors.

Because they were the only ones fit enough to walk,
Foulkes and Gregg were asked to identify those on the
stretchers. Harry Gregg pointed out Ray Wood as they were
carrying out emergency procedures on his head wound and
his eye. A nurse asked Bill Foulkes to identify a man with a
very badly injured face. The man's head was tilted awkwardly
and his bottom jaw had been pushed up through his upper
jaw and into his nose. It took some moments for Foulkes to
realise that it was little Johnny Berry. The nurse gave Foulkes
a label and pen and asked him to write Berry's name on the
label. Foulkes did as he was told and she tied it to Berry's
foot. Just then, Professor Maurer passed through the corridor
and Foulkes stopped him to ask what Berry's chances were.
"Twenty-five, seventy-five," Maurer said, "but I'm not God."
A German priest appeared and Berry was given the last rites.

Maurer moved over to Jackie Blanchflower, who was also
seemingly moments away from death. His right arm was
smashed to pieces and cut so badly that it was almost severed
from his body. He had a shattered pelvis, 13 broken ribs and

internal damage. "Fifty-fifty at best," Maurer told Gregg and Foulkes and told the priest to give Blanchflower the last rites. Busby, too, seemed about to die. His right ribs were all broken, as were his right foot and knee, and his right lung had collapsed. He was the third person to be given the last rites that afternoon.

Still the bodies came in. Waiting for his head wounds to be stitched up, but otherwise relatively unhurt, Dennis Viollet saw Frank Swift coming into the hospital on a trolley, bleeding badly. Viollet passed out at the sight of the blood pouring from Swift's mouth and was put to bed in one of the wards. One of the staff treating the injured that day was a doctor named Frank Kessel, an Austrian who was the Head of the Neurosurgical Department. In 1938, when Germany annexed Austria, Kessel fled to Manchester and spent 10 years there as a surgeon at the Royal Infirmary. He was a keen football fan and, when he saw Frank Swift, Kessel recognised him from his days watching Manchester City play at Maine Road. Pointing to Swift, Kessel said to his colleagues: "*Das ist ein Englischer Fussballspieler.*" It was only then the hospital staff knew whose lives they were desperately trying to save.

Swift was still alive when he arrived, but died minutes later. His main aorta artery had been severed – he never stood a chance. Harry Gregg remembers hearing about his death on the hospital intercom system. The hospital staff wanted Gregg, Foulkes and Charlton to lie down and rest after all three had been given injections for shock, but rather than stay amidst all the carnage and confusion of the hospital, Gregg decided to leave and Foulkes went with him. They walked quickly down the corridor, lined with patients on trolleys and stretchers and bodies covered in shrouds, and out of the hospital. Not knowing where to go, they stood on the hospital steps. It was only then that, although his clothes were relatively undamaged, Bill Foulkes noticed he only had one shoe. A blonde German woman, who was a BEA rep, appeared from nowhere and led them to the nearby Stachus Hotel. They were shown to a suite and, once ensconced in the warmth, Bill Foulkes pointed out that he only had one shoe, so the woman went off to buy a new pair for him, taking the remaining shoe as a guide to size. She returned some time later with a pair of fur-lined boots.

Because of the overwhelming numbers of injured, the procedure that day involved up to 50 nurses, most of whom were in fact nuns from the local nunnery, dressed from head to foot in black. After the initial triage in the hospital corridors, Maurer ordered the five critically injured upstairs to an operating theatre on the first floor that was doubling as a makeshift intensive care unit. Those were Matt Busby, Duncan Edwards, Ken Rayment, Johnny Berry and someone with the name 'Andrew MacDonald' scrawled in red across his exposed chest. None of the hospital staff seemed to know who he was, so someone got onto the phone to make some enquiries. During the rest of the day, the airline checked their records and confirmed that there was no crew member by the name of Andrew MacDonald on their books.

In the meantime, after early reports that he had been pulled out of the wreckage alive, Frank Taylor was still unaccounted for. As the evening wore on, it was confirmed that Frank Taylor was still missing. At home, Taylor's wife, Peggy, was fraught with worry – unlike every other wife or girlfriend, she'd had no word at all about her husband all day. Seeing that no one knew who Andrew MacDonald was, the only other alternative was that he had been allowed onto the flight at the last minute by someone in the United party. But who? Of course, many of those who possibly knew lay unconscious or dead and couldn't be asked.

Late in the night, Andrew MacDonald was taken to the operating theatre, where he underwent an operation lasting several hours. On returning to intensive care, he began to struggle with the nurses and doctor who were by his bedside. He briefly regained consciousness and was asked his name. He said his name was Frank Taylor. There was a huge sigh of relief when the hospital heard that the last remaining passenger had been accounted for. Word was sent to the *News Chronicle* back in Manchester, who were at that time busy setting the obituaries for the morning edition – they could take Taylor's obituary out, but they should also keep it to hand, just in case. The paper then rang Taylor's wife who, in her relief said that it was very like her husband not to remember his own name. At the last minute, she was able to join the BEA Mercy Flight, which had been organised for relatives of the injured and which was leaving at 9am the following morning, 7th February.

Later on, the mystery of 'Andrew MacDonald' was solved. In the early confusion of identifying the wounded as they arrived in hospital, Frank Taylor had had the name 'Andrew MacDonald' written on his chest because it was the name he had shouted out while unconscious and which a member of hospital staff had therefore identified him as. In fact, Andrew MacDonald is the name of Taylor's son. His full name, however, is Andrew MacDonald Taylor, so either Taylor had only shouted out part of his son's full name or the nurse hadn't heard or understood the whole name. Whatever the case, it was a mystery that caused a great deal of confusion for the first 12 hours after the crash.

The morning after the crash, Bobby Charlton woke up from the injections he had been given to get him through the night. Suffering from severe shock, but with only minor facial injuries, Charlton didn't know where he was at first. He found himself in a room, empty except for a young German boy, not much younger than Charlton himself. Then he remembered the previous day's events.

"I asked him if he had a paper," Charlton said, "and he showed me one which had a picture of the plane and the headline was obviously about the crash. Suddenly I wanted to know what happened, every detail. I asked about the people really quite personal to me – Tommy Taylor, David Pegg, Eddie Colman. We were all such friends, so when the German lad read out that they were all dead, I couldn't understand how I could have been 50 yards away from the aeroplane, still strapped in my seat, without suffering anything but a band on my head, which needed a few stitches. How could that be? How could I feel myself all over and find out that I was all right, completely whole and my pals were dead?" The young German boy said he was sorry. Later that day, Charlton was transferred into the downstairs room already occupied by Ken Morgans and Albert Scanlon, both of whom lay unconscious. Later still, Dennis Viollet joined them after having had a similarly disorientating experience on waking in a ward surrounding by German patients. Charlton was the only one who knew who had died and who was still living, but he was locked in silence and said nothing.

By the time the BEA Mercy Flight landed and the relatives had arrived at the Rechts der Isar Hospital, it was 6pm, a full 27 hours after the crash. Teresa Foulkes and Mavis Gregg, who were close friends, had both wanted to come to see their husbands but the husbands refused point blank. "You're not flying. You're not flying out here, you're not doing it," Harry Gregg told his wife. The last thing either husband wanted his wife to do was fly on an aeroplane. The scene awaiting those relatives who did fly was one of total devastation. Upstairs in the intensive care unit, the five most seriously wounded people still lay unconscious.

In the dim light of the operating theatre, Peggy Taylor stood by her husband's side. A tube came out of Taylor's left foot and another was clamped to his nose. When she asked the nurse keeping watch over Taylor what her husband's chances were, the nurse held out her hands, like a set of scales, to indicate that it was fifty-fifty. As is often the case when the body undergoes massive injury and shock, a secondary complication had developed – in Taylor's case he had contracted pneumonia and the next few hours were critical.

By Matt Busby's bed was his wife, Jean. A plastic oxygen tent had been erected around his bed and he was breathing through a tube. So severe were his chest and lung injuries that Busby was operated on for five hours immediately after the crash and given a tracheotomy to enable him to breathe. He lay in a deep coma and the battle to save his life had continued into the night. But he wasn't expected to survive, so a Catholic priest had already administered the last rites, again. Doctor Kessel told Jean Busby that "every minute that we manage to keep life in him is precious." Before the arrival of the relatives, the doctors at the hospital had organised every English-speaking member of staff to stay near the bedsides of those gravely ill in case they had any last messages for their loved ones. Every time Busby stirred, a nurse would lean over him and whisper into his ear: "Mr Busby, Mr Busby. You must listen and live. Your family is coming to see you. Please listen."

Johnny Berry and Ken Rayment were also both in comas. Ken Rayment had received bad injuries to his head, which had been shaved in order to be operated on. Johnny Berry had a fractured skull, broken jaw, mouth injuries so bad that all his teeth had to be removed, a shattered elbow joint and broken pelvis. Wires and tubes came out of him from top to toe and the doctors gave him little chance of surviving. Despite, or perhaps because of, the severity of Berry's injuries, Berry's wife, Hilda, was one whose calm in the face of such dreadful adversity deeply impressed the other relatives. Next to Johnny Berry lay Duncan Edwards, who was also in an oxygen tent. Edwards's injuries seemed, on the face of it, less severe than Busby's, but they were in fact more serious. Although he was conscious and alert for a few days after the crash, while Busby slipped in and out of consciousness, Edwards had suffered terrible damage internally, especially to his kidneys. A kidney machine was being flown from Stuttgart to Munich to better treat his injuries. He had broken ribs, a broken pelvis, a collapsed lung and pneumothorax. His right thigh had multiple fractures as well. His parents and his fiancée, Molly Leach, stayed with him. Although Edwards remained awake and chatted to them, Professor Maurer said his chances were no more than fifty-fifty.

Albert Scanlon says: "Except for Blanchy, the boss and [Frank] Taylor and Johnny Berry, I was injured more than anybody. I was actually injured more than Duncan, but Duncan had the injuries inside him and Duncan died after fifteen days or summat like that. And yet I'd spoke to Duncan in the hospital. I'd gone up with Ray Wood and we'd seen him. Johnny Berry we couldn't speak to because Johnny was out of the game, but we spoke to Duncan and he was surrounded. The day he died I was up there and the operating theatre they had him in, it was surrounded by nuns, they was all in the habits, they was all in black, and he was on twenty-four hour care. Duncan did some roaring and shouting. Duncan was playing football matches while he was in hospital. You know, if you're in pain and you get a visitor like Jimmy visiting and one of the questions Duncan says, 'What time are we playing these Wolves?' – that was the next match – and he was still in that position where he remembered that he was going to play Wolves on the Saturday."

At first, Albert Scanlon himself had looked in very bad shape. Harry Gregg remembers seeing him lying on the ground under one of the wheels covered in blood and with a gaping wound to his skull. But after an operation to close his wound and after being cleaned up, his injuries were far less serious than first supposed. He had his arm and leg set in plaster and his head covered in bandages, but he would recover. When he was admitted to the hospital, however, Scanlon did some roaring and shouting of his own. Scanlon takes up the story:

"There was one particular day and the door opened, it was an afternoon, and Sister Almunder, she was a little plump woman, always laughing, and behind her was a tall woman, a nun and their [convent] provided the hospital with the majority of the nurses, and she was dressed all in black. And she kept coming across, and I had bandages across me head and all this plaster, and she kept coming across and laughing. And they'd be chuckling away in German. Anyway, she was there about ten minutes and she come and she patted me head and she went off. And she stopped at the door and looked and then went off. So Father O'Hagan come in and I said, 'Listen, I've had a nun come in with Sister Almunder and she kept looking and touching me and… he says 'She's going on holiday'. I said, 'What d'you mean?' and he says, 'They go to the mother [superior's] house for a holiday, but in case you went out, she wanted to see what you was like when you weren't fighting'. And I said, 'What you mean, fighting?' And he says, 'Well when they was operating on your skull, she lay on you through the operation, holding your arms down, but she lay across your, your top and you punched her, you swore at her', he says 'apparently it all come out about your divorce', and they were mopping her head and they were mopping mine – they were doing me skull, here, 'cos it was wide open. And all the way through the operation she was the one that lay on me and held me down so I wouldn't get up and fight and all like that. But he says, 'What come out of your mouth, you were calling her everything and she was going away, a fortnight's holiday and she wanted to see what you was like before, in case she went away and come back and you'd gone'. And that girl had lay across me about four hours while they did me operation."

Also on board the Mercy Flight was Jimmy Murphy. When he arrived in Munich, Murphy went straight to the Stachus

Hotel, checked in and met up with Bill Foulkes and Harry Gregg. High on Murphy's list of priorities was to start looking after those who had survived by showing his face around the hospital and keeping spirits up. Gregg says: "[Jimmy Murphy's] the one that said to Bill Foulkes and myself when he arrived the day after the crash, he said, 'Can you go down to the hospital with us?' He was the one that said, 'If some of the lads see you, they'll not know how bad it is'. Cos some of the lads was conscious and we did the rounds for him. And he kept us there for two or three days so that those that were conscious would see us."

Murphy did the rounds at the hospital, looking in on Bobby Charlton, Dennis Viollet, Ken Morgans and Albert Scanlon, who were still in the same room together. Charlton was being kept in for observation. Viollet had a nasty gash in his head and facial injuries but, like Charlton, his injuries were not serious or life-threatening. Although Scanlon still lay in a coma, and would do so for six days after the crash, he didn't look too bad given his injuries and had been given the thumbs up by Maurer. Ken Morgans, the right-winger who'd only just got into the first team, was also still in a coma and had been ever since the crash two days previously. Morgans was the last person to be pulled out of the wreckage. On the day of the crash, he was only found by chance four hours afterwards because a German reporter went back to the wreckage to look for the newsreel canisters and happened to find Morgans groaning amongst the piles of luggage. He didn't have a scratch on him but the impact of the crash had sent his body into deep shock.

Gregg went in to see his old friend, Jackie Blanchflower, in Room 406. "I watched Jean Blanchflower break down in the room – there was a shoe lying in the corner 'cos I'd had picked up that shoe in the mud and the shit, I put it on my foot, it was three sizes too big 'cos I have small feet. And I said,

'I picked that bloody thing up in the snow' and she started to scream, 'That was Jackie's shoe!'."

When Bill Foulkes visited Frank Taylor in the operating theatre, he was conscious and in relatively good spirits, pointing at his leg in plaster and joking that he was having a smashing time. Each of the players had their own nun to look after them – Taylor's nun was called Sister Solemnis. Taylor asked her to bring them some beer, to which she wagged an admonishing finger and said no, but Professor Maurer interceded and said that it would be alright as long as it was only a small amount. After Taylor had his sip of beer, Foulkes asked him if he knew where all the other players were being kept because he and Gregg wanted to say hello, but Taylor didn't know. Foulkes turned to Sister Solemnis and asked her which hospital he and Gregg should go to next in order to see the other players, but the Sister shook her head. "This is it," she said. "There is no other hospital". Foulkes asked where Bert Whalley and Tom Curry were, but the nurse just shook her head. Only then did Foulkes really start to comprehend the magnitude of the disaster.

For two days after the crash, Harry Gregg and Bill Foulkes went back and forth from the Stachus Hotel to the hospital, visiting the players in an attempt at keeping spirits high but, now that they were beginning to realise the truth, a gap was opening up inside them, between the knowledge they had about the condition of those still in hospital and the progress they would themselves make compared to the others. Aside from the difficulty of dealing with such grief on their own and so far from home, it was only going to become more difficult for them to hide the truth from the others. Murphy wisely realised that the time was right for them to go home. That weekend, with Murphy accompanying them, Gregg and Foulkes caught an overnight train called the Rheingold Express bound for the Hook of Holland via Frankfurt, Cologne and Rotterdam.

After their departure, Ken Morgans came round. "I woke on the Sunday," Morgans says, "and we weren't told about the players that had died until days later. 'Cos the professor of the hospital, he wouldn't allow anybody to tell us about the players that had died, you know. So we thought they might have been upstairs, 'cos there was a few players that were upstairs. I think it was a lot of days afterwards that the professor came in and told us."

Lying next to him, Bobby Charlton, for one, was hugely relieved that Morgans hadn't died. Charlton could no longer remember the names of the dead that the German boy with the newspaper had read out. Somehow, his brain had prevented him from knowing. "I just didn't remember," he has said, "I didn't know what had happened. Obviously, people lying in the snow, that stays with you, but maybe grasping it was all too much." His mind just couldn't process the information – something that bothered Charlton greatly. Despite the mental troubles he was having, however, Charlton was physically quite well and he left hospital a week after the crash.

Before he left the hospital, however, he wanted to say goodbye to one person in particular. He went upstairs to the operating theatre where Duncan Edwards lay in bed, hooked up to an artificial kidney. Edwards happened to be conscious at the time and shouted at Charlton: "Where the bloody hell have you been?" Edwards and Charlton had done their National Service together in Shropshire and Edwards had shouted the same question to Charlton when he was late one day.

Having said his goodbyes, Charlton travelled back to England, also on the Rheingold Express, arriving back in England on St Valentine's Day. At London's Liverpool Street Station, his brother, Jack, and his mother were waiting for him. They made the extremely long journey by road to the family home in Ashington, in the north-east. Neither his brother nor mother asked him anything about the crash, knowing full well to leave him alone. No one said much of anything and there were long periods of silence. Eventually, Charlton turned to them and said he knew they wanted to hear about what happened and so he was going to tell them just this once and then he didn't want to talk about it anymore. He told them everything that he could remember about the air crash and the hospital and didn't speak about it again.

On the Monday morning after the crash, Busby and Frank Taylor were taken off the critical list and moved that day out of intensive care and into another room. It was a memorable day for them as Maurer told them that, although they were still very ill and would be in hospital for a long time, he was now sure that they would eventually recover. Busby was wheeled in his stainless steel bed out of the operating theatre, along the corridor through a series of frosted-glass double doors and into Room 401, in the part of the hospital that Maurer had sectioned off for private patients.

It was also a memorable day because it was unseasonably warm. A mini heatwave had descended upon Munich, prompting Busby to ask for the doors in his room overlooking the garden to be opened and his bed to be wheeled out onto the balcony. When all this was done for him, Busby gazed up at the clear blue, cloudless sky for a few moments. It was simply too blue to be real and Busby said, "Get me back in, get me back in". The next morning, it started snowing again.

Frank Taylor was also moved that morning to Room 401. In his book *The Day a Team Died*, he describes the room: "There was ample room for two beds, a wash basin with concealed lighting in a recess, built-in wardrobes for two; on each bed a flexible reading light; the large light in the ceiling shielded to prevent the glare being thrown into a sick person's eyes and in the wall by each bed an oxygen cylinder... On the further side of the room facing the door, the wall was perhaps only 2 ft. 6 in. high. Above that nothing but plate glass for the entire length of the room. In the cosseted life of the hospital, a somewhat monastic unreal existence, the patient could see the clustered rooftops of Munich, the Bavarian State Parliament Building and the steeple of St John's Church, while down in the roads there was the busy clatter of the trams, the honking of cars, the hustle and bustle of people."

For four days, Taylor looked out the window or stared at the sky-blue wall opposite his bed. When he wasn't doing that, he looked at Matt Busby's inert form in bed, occasionally throwing a comment his way, but there was hardly any response. Busby was once again inside an oxygen tent. A doctor was constantly on hand treating him and his nun, Sister Gilda, the Chief Nursing Sister in the hospital, was forever hovering around the bed. His foot had to be re-broken and set in plaster, but Maurer couldn't put Busby under general anaesthetic because of the injuries to his chest, so they had to do it without. Busby never complained, just coughed once or twice.

Then, all of a sudden, Taylor was moved out of Room 401 to Room 406, the room Jackie Blanchflower was in. The doctors told Taylor that Busby needed complete solitude. Despite being sure to recover, Busby was still in such a bad way that he would need complete silence and round-the-clock medical attention. Taylor was sad to be leaving Busby, but he realised his efforts to chat with him was probably the reason he was being transferred. Three nuns were needed to move Taylor – two to lift him onto a bed with wheels and one to hold up his right leg, which was surrounded by a metal cage in order to keep the sheets of it. He was a bag of bones. The nurses wheeled him further down the corridor and put him to a bed opposite Blanchflower.

Although Busby and Taylor were just starting on the road to recovery, Jackie Blanchflower was nowhere near to being past the worst yet. Like Busby, he was a shadow of his former self. His injuries were not initially deemed to be as serious as those of the five who were put into intensive care, but over the first few days after the crash Blanchflower's condition deteriorated and he was put on the critical list. Maurer and his staff weren't sure, but they suspected he might have suffered damage to his kidneys, as Edwards had.

While all this was going on in the private patients' section of the hospital, back in the intensive care unit, Edwards' condition had deteriorated suddenly and alarmingly six days after the crash. Maurer had to perform a six-hour emergency operation in order to try to save his life. It worked, but Edwards was now more ill than ever. Maurer said it would be at least five years before Edwards would be able to use his right leg again even if he did recover from his injuries, which he now thought was a 25% chance, at best. Busby still had no idea of the full extent of the tragedy but, even so, Maurer instructed his staff again that under no circumstances was anyone to mention who had died or discuss anyone's chances of survival to Matt Busby or anyone else who was still seriously ill.

And then, amidst the gloom, there was some good news – Albert Scanlon regained consciousness. When she saw him, Sister Almunder said "Ah, Mr Scanlon, it's nice to see you awake. It's the first time I've seen you conscious in the six days you've been here." This was a relief for Dennis Viollet and Ken Morgans because they were both confined to their beds and had had no one to talk to for days, ever since Jimmy Murphy, Harry Gregg and Bill Foulkes and then Bobby Charlton had left and gone back to England.

It wasn't long before they kicked off with their old jokes and routines. Because he was going through a messy divorce, Scanlon got it the worst. The other two ribbed him constantly about it. It killed the time. They were always looking to play practical jokes on each other, too. Morgans remembers one played on Ray Wood, who was in a room next to theirs.

Wood had facial injuries and had banged his head very
badly, resulting in concussion, acute tinnitus and double vision,
but the most serious injury he suffered was to his right leg,
which was broken in several places. Wood had his leg up in
traction and couldn't move a muscle. When a nun came into
their room carrying a set of long needles used in deep lumbar
injections, they told her to go next door into Wood's room.
They all knew that Wood was absolutely terrified of needles.
"No, no," the sister said, "I'm not going to that room", but
they insisted: "Yes, yes, you go into that room and just say, 'Mr
Wood?'". Looking slightly confused, the sister did as she was
asked, and when she disappeared through the door to Ray
Wood's room, the three of them broke into laughter.

Those that were getting better were astounded at the
treatment they received at the Rechts der Isar Hospital. The
hospital was more like a hotel, with a quality of food to match.
You could order "anything you wanted," Morgans says. "You
had steak, it was always on a wooden plate, I don't know
why. Always on a wooden plate. Champagne. And we had
this amazing chocolate cake. Never tasted a chocolate cake
before or since like it. Oh, this chocolate cake was wonderful
chocolate cake, layers and layers of cream, white cream. About
eight layers of chocolate and about eight layers of cream. It
was fantastic, absolutely fantastic."

They also had a big barrel of lager, sent to them by the
American forces based in Germany, who also sent them dozens
of cartons of cigarettes. "Three Irish girls come from the
American forces, and they brought us a trunk and it was as big
as that and it was nothing but cigarettes and books," Scanlon
says. "Also the British army sent one, they were the same." In
addition to that, the players received the rather unlikely gift
of a crate of gorgonzola cheese. Albert Scanlon tells the story:

"My nun was a little plump girl, Sister Almunder and she
says to us one day, 'My father, who was a billionaire, and he'd

two sons and a daughter…' she was the daughter, and when she insisted she was gonna be a nun, he split his fortune up three ways and he give her her share and then that went to the monastery. And she told us what to eat, Wiener Schnitzel and all that, and she'd say if it was good or not. And she come in this one day and she says, 'My father, or Papa, says you can have anything you want, anything you want'. Well we'd got these cigs and we'd got fruit and Dennis says, 'We'll have some Coca-Cola'. So she says, 'Yeah'. So we said, 'Yeah, we'll have a Coca-Cola, bring us some Coca-Cola'. So the next day these two chaps come in brown coats and they put this trunk down and after about an hour Dennis got up and said, 'D'you want a drink?' I was in the next bed to Dennis. And he went and opened this trunk and he's looking and I says, 'What is it?' And he says, 'What it is? It's gorgonzola cheese', it was a trunk full of gorgonzola cheese. So we got her and she's going on and her dad, this fellow appeared the same afternoon, he was immaculate and he could speak English and he said, 'I'm sorry about that'."

These gifts were shared with the players' wives and girlfriends, all of whom were still there, staying in hotels and coming into the hospital every day. Barbara, Dennis Viollet's wife, Albert Scanlon's wife, Josie (even though they were divorcing) and Ray Wood's wife, Betty and even Duncan Edwards' girlfriend, Molly, used to come to visit. All the wives and girlfriends had been asked not to talk about what had happened and so, although they laughed and joked with the players, they avoided talking about what was going on upstairs. But, the truth of the matter is that the players weren't in a hurry to ask. Scanlon: "The thing is, you're in a hospital bed or ward and you got Kenny Morgans, Ray Wood and the pilot. And you've got Dennis Viollet and me and you don't mention the others, because you think if they mention that Duncan and Johnny's up above, you think the rest of them are up above, because you're seeing Mr and Mrs Edwards.

It's the first time I ever met Mr and Mrs Blanchflower. You see Jean, Josie was there, Betty Wood, Dennis's wife, this pilot's missus and you see Mr and Mrs Edwards, Mrs Berry and her mother. You see Mr and Mrs Bent, the mother and father, but these people were dead. Mr and Mrs Colman, they was all there and yet you're afraid to ask."

Gradually, the health of the players downstairs began to improve significantly, all under the so ever watchful eye of Professor Maurer. Pretty soon, Dennis Viollet was up and about on his own two feet, as were Albert Scanlon and Ray Wood, albeit only in wheelchairs. Back in England, United were about to play their first game since the Munich crash – Sheffield Wednesday at Old Trafford, the fifth round FA Cup tie they had heard being drawn live on the radio the morning of their departure to Belgrade. That morning now seemed aeons away. Scanlon says: "Me and Dennis, when they played Sheffield Wednesday, the first match after the crash, it was a cup tie, me and Dennis could get out. And on the other side of the ward was a little office, all glass, and they had two phones directly through to Old Trafford, so we listened to the match." Every five minutes, Viollet would run around the ward, relaying to everyone else what had happened.

United won 3-0. The atmosphere at Old Trafford that night was one of the strangest ever experienced at the ground. For the crowd, there was a sense of great sadness, but also a pride and a determination, one that occasionally spilled over into an extraordinary kind of elation. For Harry Gregg and Bill Foulkes, who played that night as goalkeeper and right-back respectively, the result meant very little. It was an occasion filled only with sadness and they were completely drained afterwards. For Viollet, listening to the game and hearing the roar of the crowd had made him realise just how homesick he was.

For Scanlon, it was also a strange experience, but not because of how the game made him feel, but because of a peculiar moment unfolding in front of his eyes during the course of the game: "Next door to us from outside they brought this chap in and they brought this woman and her kids while we were watching the match and they were gypsies. And he was sat on a commode, this gypsy, and we actually watched him die during the match. He finished up trying to eat the commode and he was sat there and they were still sat outside when we were watching him perform on this commode, and he died, and that was during the game." This bizarre episode showed how brutal life could be inside a hospital.

Scanlon remembers that "Sister Almunder used to take me everywhere in a wheelchair and Woody'd be in a wheelchair and his nun was a bit older. And the thing was, we used to race to the chapel and we'd race round the hospital." Sister Almunder also put Scanlon in the lift and took him upstairs to see the others. Of the seven United players left in the hospital two weeks after the crash, three were still seriously ill upstairs: Duncan Edwards, Johnny Berry and Jackie Blanchflower. Johnny Berry and Duncan Edwards were comatose – Berry had been ever since the crash. Scanlon looked in on them, then went into Room 406 and saw Jackie Blanchflower too, but although Blanchflower was conscious, he was too ill to talk. Scanlon then went in to see Busby and noticed that Busby's sandy-coloured hair had turned white. Looking at Busby's inert body in the bed, it was then, he says, that the tragedy really hit home.

Dennis Viollet also went upstairs to see the boss. "How are the rest of the boys?" Busby asked, but Viollet didn't really know – the staff and relatives had followed Maurer's appeals and withheld the worst of the news from all the survivors. Instead, he talked about the victory over Sheffield Wednesday and who United's possible opponents could be in the sixth round, but Busby didn't seem that interested in talking about football. In fact, he had said several times to his wife in the days and weeks after the crash that he wanted nothing more to do with football ever again.

But worse was still to come for Busby. Two days after the Sheffield Wednesday game, and 15 days after the crash, Duncan Edwards died in the early hours of the morning of 21st February. Maurer and his staff at the hospital had been deeply impressed by his will to live and the extent to which his spirit had struggled to survive. It had been a monumental battle. Given the number and severity of his injuries, it was incredible even to have survived for as long as he had. "I do not think anyone other than this young man could have survived so long," said Maurer, "his resistance made us admire him." Edwards was a Colossus of football and if there was one player who represented everything the Busby Babes stood for – youth, team spirit, talent, grit, loyalty, glory – it was Edwards.

Busby was still a very vulnerable patient. His injuries were severe but, as it was certain now that he would eventually recover, much more significant was his mental health. He blamed himself entirely for the Munich Air Crash and carried that blame heavily. Of course, no one around him blamed Busby at all, but that was the kind of man Busby was – he placed the burden of responsibility for everything to do with the club squarely on his own shoulders. He wouldn't hear of it any other way.

Maurer and the rest of the staff endeavoured to keep the news of Edwards' death from Busby. A blanket of silence was wrapped around him. But they knew he would have to be told sooner or later. His wife Jean stepped up to the mark and said that, when the time was right, she would tell him. There was such a hushed atmosphere as the doctors and nurses went about their business that Busby began to sense that something was wrong, dreadfully wrong, but he was too afraid to ask.

Days passed, snow kept falling from the plaster-white skies and the medical care continued round the clock. For six days, the staff struggled to hide the awful truth, but then Busby overheard a visiting German priest inadvertently letting it slip that Edwards was dead. For the first time, Busby said later, the reality of what had happened finally dawned on him. The worst thing in the world had actually happened. He knew then that there must have been many more deaths and that this was what he sensed everyone was keeping from him. That evening, his wife Jean and children, Sheena and Sandy, were by his bedside, as usual. They were not talking much – there was nothing much to say. Busby turned to them and said that he knew about Duncan and that he wanted them to tell him the truth. They tried to change the subject, but Busby insisted. For his own peace of mind, he said, he needed to know. Jean knew that the moment had come and took his hand in hers. When Busby called out the names one by one, Jean either nodded and squeezed his hand or else shook her head. When Busby realised how many had died, he lay back and wept.

The awful news, together with the dawning reality that he was going to have to face the families of those who had died, sent him into a deep depression. For three days afterwards, he hardly spoke a word or ate a thing. The same questions went round and round in his mind: "Why didn't I die with them? What's so special about me?" Like Bobby Charlton, Busby was beginning to develop the guilt from which survivors of terrible accidents suffer. Most of all, he still blamed himself for taking the young players out to Belgrade in the first place. If he hadn't done that, they would all still be alive. Torturing himself in this way, Busby spiralled into a pit of despair.

Three weeks after the crash, Ray Wood was deemed fit enough to leave. Of all who had survived, there were now six patients left in the Rechts der Isar Hospital: Busby, Jackie Blanchflower, Ken Morgans, Albert Scanlon, Frank Taylor and Dennis Viollet. Like Edwards, Ken Rayment's fight for life was sadly to end in defeat. He never regained consciousness and died around the same time as Edwards. Busby was moved out of Room 401 to a room further along the corridor, while Frank Taylor and Blanchflower were moved back into Room 401, where they would remain for the rest of their stay in hospital.

By now, the two men had spent a great deal of time together and had got to know each other pretty well. A familiar routine had developed. Every day at six o'clock in the morning, Sister Solemnis would enter the room and, in faultless English, would say "Good morning, Mr Taylor. Did you sleep well? Any pains during the night?" Coming to his bedside with a bowl of warm water, she would then wash his face, chest, his left arm (the right was in plaster) and left leg. Blanchflower was usually still asleep during all this – he had difficulty falling asleep at night and so the nuns would let him rest for a little while longer. At 7:30 on the dot, Sister Gilda, wearing her brilliant white cap, would come in, saying "Come on, Jackie. Wakey, wakey." Taylor found this very amusing.

After a breakfast of soft-boiled eggs and tea, either with lemon or peppermint, Maurer would stride in, "like a sergeant-major" Taylor said, the first of three visits per day. He brought with him a stainless steel trolley on which was a vast array of scalpels, forceps and other surgical instruments. Very carefully, he began working on Taylor's right leg, clearing out bits of dirt and metal.

Taylor wasn't aware of it at the time, but his right leg was in constant danger of having to be amputated throughout the weeks and months following the crash. During one of these close inspections, he overheard Maurer using the word 'infection' to one of the nurses helping him. Taylor was horrified, but too afraid to ask how serious it was. That night, Taylor lay wide-awake, worrying what was going to happen and how he would cope without the use of his leg. In the morning, no sooner had his wife, Peggy, come to visit him as usual than Taylor admitted his fear to her. "Don't let them do it to me, please," he said, "I know the truth about my leg. It's infected, but please ask if it is gangrene." His wife looked at him. "What about your friends George Fellows, Henry Rose and Eric Thompson – aren't you forgetting them?" she said, "they are not here to complain. You ought to realise how thankful we all are that you are alive. Both your arm and leg are infected but it is not gangrene. The doctors have assured me of that." Taylor felt chastised by his wife, but deep down he knew she was right and he was grateful for her perspective.

On 1st March, United played West Bromwich Albion at The Hawthorns in the sixth round of the FA Cup. The hospital staff had once again hooked up a telephone feed from Old Trafford so that Dennis Viollet and Albert Scanlon could listen to the match. It was only then they heard that, less than a month after the crash, Bobby Charlton would be playing for the first time since his return to England. It was a peculiar feeling for Viollet and Scanlon. They were so far from home and desperate to get back, and yet here was their close friend and team mate playing for United again in a cup tie. United drew 2-2. The moment emphasised how much distance there was between themselves and their old lives. How would things be when they finally returned to England? Something had changed for them and they weren't sure if they'd ever get it back.

Viollet was much improved by now and had actually been discharged from the hospital a few days earlier, but he had to return every day for treatment as an outpatient. The real reason the hospital were keeping him on, however, was that Ken Morgans was almost ready to be discharged too and Maurer wanted Viollet and his wife Barbara to wait so that Morgans could travel back with them. Morgans' girlfriend, Stephanie, had not come out to Munich because she was still living in Wales at the time and hadn't had enough direct contact with the club for it to arrange a visa for her to fly out to Munich. Maurer did not want any of the survivors to travel alone so it was decided that Viollet and his wife would wait until Morgans was well enough to travel with them.

On 5th March, Morgans was finally well enough to leave hospital and travel home. Ironically, it was the day that United had their cup tie replay against West Bromwich Albion, this time at Old Trafford. As they had done with every member of the United party returning to England, BEA offered to fly them home, but Morgans and Viollet also chose to go overnight on the Rheingold Express, following the same route Harry Gregg and Bill Foulkes had travelled nearly a month previously. When they woke up the next morning in England, one of the train's stewards served them breakfast and told them that United had scored in the 90th minute and won 1–0. For Viollet and Morgans, it was the best welcome home present they could have had.

Albert Scanlon was now all by himself in the downstairs room, but he still had cigarettes and the gorgonzola cheese to barter with: "I was the last man in our ward, everybody had gone and I used to sleep sat up because of me arm in plaster and me body was in plaster and all this leg was in plaster and I was dozing this one weekend, just had the one little light on and the bed went down and I looked up and there was a nurse sat there. And she says, 'Can I have some cigarettes?' We used to give 'em to the nurses like. So I said, 'Yeah, go and get…' and she got a packet out. And I said, 'No, take the carton'. She says, 'They're only for me papa'. So I says, 'No, take the carton'. Couldn't move, and she sat on the bed and every one of her teeth was silver, I think she was Romanian or Bulgarian, and they're all silver and she's saying, 'Yeah?' I says, 'Yeah, take the cigarettes'. And she put the cigarettes down and started opening her jumper. And she went like, took it off, so she's got her bust, and I'm saying, 'No, no' and she's saying, 'Yeah, for the cigarettes, you have me' and all like this. And I say it took me about quarter of an hour of saying 'I can't move'. And I never seen her again, but she knew we had the cigarettes, 'cos we told them if ever they wanted any, come. But she was willing to give herself to me because I give her two hundred cigarettes for her dad. She just sat down and started undoing her buttons and I thought, if this plaster wasn't on you would never have got off the bed, but I can't move. And I never seen her again."

Incredibly, soon after this incident, Scanlon himself was deemed sufficiently recovered by Maurer to be allowed home. None of the others still in the hospital would be well enough to be discharged for some time and so, rather than hang around waiting for them, Scanlon decided to travel by himself. He had to leave hospital wearing a pair of carpet slippers because his feet were still in plaster. Dressing him in trousers, the nuns had to cut the sides open to get his plastered legs in. He left the hospital with no belongings, taking the Rheingold Express home as well.

Meanwhile, the 7th March was Jackie Blanchflower's 25th birthday. While he was still sleeping, Sisters Gilda and Solemnis crept into Room 401, with an enormous birthday cake they had ordered from the hospital bakery. They decorated a table and put the cake on it, then waved the other nurses and hospital orderlies into the room. Standing around his bed, they started to sing 'Happy Birthday'. What a wonderful sight it must have been for Blanchflower when he woke and saw the cake in front of him. Blanchflower rubbed his eyes and thanked them. He didn't know what else to say.

A few days later, after four and a half long weeks in a deep coma, Johnny Berry finally came round. It was a very happy moment for Maurer and his staff. Because Berry had been so close to death for so long and because they had lost both Edwards and Rayment after long battles, Berry's recovery meant a great deal to them.

The day Berry came round, it just so happened that his former captain at United, Johnny Carey, had flown to Munich and was in the hospital to see Matt Busby. Carey had waited so long before coming to see his old boss because he thought that Busby would rather be with his family until he was well enough to see old friends. When he heard that Berry was conscious, Carey raced upstairs to see him and then got Berry into a wheelchair and pushed the little right-winger around the corridors. Berry came up to see the boss and complained that his best friend Tommy Taylor hadn't been in to see him. Just as he had with other survivors who would eventually recover but who were not yet out of danger, Maurer had ordered a curtain of silence to be drawn around Berry until he was mentally strong enough to bear the strain of hearing the truth of the crash. Busby looked at the genuinely puzzled Berry and realised again the magnitude of the task ahead – facing those people whose lives had been altered forever by the tragedy. It was almost too much for Busby – he later said that Berry's remark was the lowest point of his recovery.

Although he was still sunk in a black depression, Busby knew that, sooner or later, he was going to have to face the loved ones of the players he had lost. At this time, Busby was well enough to be on his feet for a few minutes a day and, now that he was physically a bit better, Busby felt it was his duty to speak to them. He owed it to them – it was the very least he could do. He asked for a phone to be put in his room and began calling each player's wife or girlfriend. When he spoke to Eddie Colman's girlfriend, Marjorie, he broke down and wept. He told Geoff Bent's wife, Marion, that he blamed himself for allowing the players back onto the plane. Talking to the women only made matters worse. Why should he think at all about returning to football? After everything that had happened, it seemed wrong somehow. Sensing his despondency, Jean Busby said, "I'm sure those who have gone would have wanted you to carry on." It was a comment that he very much took to heart and, from that moment on, Matt Busby turned a corner and finally began the long and arduous process of regaining his will to live.

Six gruelling weeks after the crash, Jackie Blanchflower was at last strong enough to leave the Rechts der Isar Hospital. It was another victory for Maurer and his staff. The damage to Blanchflower's kidneys was not, after all, as serious as Maurer had thought. The terrible injury to his right arm, however, still caused him pain and he received treatment on it for the rest of his life. His arm was so badly injured that it was operated on several occasions, the last being 1974, a full sixteen years after the crash. He and his wife, Jean, caught the Belgrade Express train to Calais and sailed on to Dover, where there was a taxi waiting to take them to Manchester. On the way, the driver turned on the radio to listen to that Wednesday night's football game. Once again, somewhat ironically, Blanchflower happened to be travelling at the same time that United were playing a huge match. Blanchflower knew perfectly well what game it was: the FA Cup semi-final replay against Fulham after a 2-2 draw, in which Charlton had scored both goals, but Blanchflower wasn't interested in it. It just reminded him of all his friends that were dead and gone, particularly Tommy Taylor, who had been like another brother to him. He didn't care if he never played again. It would be a long drive home.

Back in Rechts der Isar Hospital, however, the game was met with a great deal more enthusiasm. Via a telephone feed, Frank Taylor's colleagues in England had arranged for Taylor to have a "ball-by-ball" account of United's game. Taylor listened intently as United went ahead twice only for Fulham to draw level both times. Midway through the second half, Professor Kessel came into Room 401 after finishing an operation. "Is our team winning?" he said and listened as Taylor gave him a commentary on the game. United scored again to go 3-2 up.

A few minutes later, they scored again! Surely it was game over, but Fulham pulled one back. Kessel listened in agony, waiting for the final whistle. Then, in the final minute of the game, Bobby Charlton scored from a volley outside the box. 5-3! United had done it! Professor Kessel rushed out of the room to tell Maurer and his other colleagues the news. Unbelievably, just seven weeks after the Munich Air Disaster, a team cobbled together out of crash survivors, a few young, inexperienced reserves and one or two players hurriedly bought from other clubs was in the final of the FA Cup.

When he was told the news, it was like a shot in the arm for Matt Busby. He had slowly begun to take an interest in football again. After the disastrous FA Cup Final the previous year against Aston Villa – the game in which Ray Wood's jaw had been broken – he and the captain, Roger Byrne, had promised the fans that United would return to Wembley the following year. True to form, their word was kept, but Byrne wouldn't be there to play. Busby tried not to think about that. It would take a long time before he attained his former enthusiasm for the game, but it would come, eventually. For now, Busby looked ahead. The FA Cup Final against Bolton Wanderers was on 3rd May. He decided he would try to be well enough to watch the game at Wembley.

Busby kept his promise to himself. On 19th April, Matt Busby, accompanied by his wife Jean left the Rechts der Isar Hospital after 10 punishing and painful weeks. He was pale and unsteady on his legs – even with sticks, he could walk no further than ten yards before he had to sit down. Before leaving, he called in on Frank Taylor. Understanding one another perfectly well after ten weeks in the same awful predicament, they didn't need to say much. Busby said "See you back in Manchester" and he was off to catch the overnight Rheingold Express, a large group of photographers and pressmen in his wake, all gathered to cover the Boss' return.

Frank Taylor felt terribly lonely after Busby's departure. He was now the only patient remaining from the original United delegation to Belgrade (Johnny Berry had left some days before). The next day, Taylor received a cable from the Hook of Holland. It was from Busby and read: "*Get stripped son. You're on next.*" It did a great deal to revive his spirits.

In all, Taylor was to spend another eleven weeks at the Rechts der Isar Hospital. Once the infection in his leg cleared up, Maurer informed Taylor that he was ready to be operated on. Taylor hadn't realised that he would need another operation, so Maurer explained the situation to him. The wounds in his leg were so extensive that they would remain open and the only way to make them heal was to apply a skin graft to the leg. With a covering of skin, the tissue would have a chance to regenerate itself and, eventually close the wound. Broken bones could also be mended in this way. Until very recently, the only course of action would have been amputation, but skin grafting was now an alternative. Nevertheless, Taylor's leg was far from certain of being saved and Maurer explained that he would need several skin grafts and therefore several more operations before his leg could be saved.

Taylor's wife had flown home to be with their children, so Taylor was on his own. He was visited three times a week by Father O'Hagen, and Frank Kessel stopped by in his room regularly. Kessel often asked about Manchester, how much it had changed, if certain places were still there. These conversations were vital to Taylor on his road to recovery and they helped to form a very deep and lasting friendship between the two men. On one occasion, Taylor thanked Kessel for everything the staff at the Rechts der Isar had done for him and the others. Kessel waved his thanks aside. "We did nothing," he said, "Nothing at all that would not have been done in an English hospital in the same circumstances. Medicine is international, it was our duty to do what little we could. You must never forget a great deal depends on the patient – and some of these British boys have been absolutely wonderful. No fuss, no bother, real British phlegm in very difficult circumstances."

Spring arrived in Munich. The snow had finally stopped and the sun came out. Most days, Taylor was wheeled out onto his balcony, which ran the length of the building. On every other balcony, patients sunned themselves and breathed in the fresh air. Below them, orderlies and staff took their breaks outside, standing together in their white uniforms talking and smoking. Everything had started to turn green. Buds were bursting out on the trees, on the extensive lawns, flowers began blooming and the ducks returned to the pond, one which Taylor had heard much about but had never seen. Beyond the perimeters of the hospital was the sound of traffic – cars and tram bells. Over the city rooftops and beyond the enormous spire of St John's were the snow-capped peaks of the Bavarian Alps.

April turned into May and then May turned into June. It wouldn't be long, Maurer said, before Taylor was sufficiently recovered to travel. He had already taken a few steps with the aid of crutches, Sister Gilda and Kessel behind him in case he fell. Finally, on 2nd July, he was ready to leave. His wife had flown over to accompany him home – they would follow the by now well-worn train journey back to England via the Hook of Holland. Taylor said goodbye to Sister Solemnis, Kessel and Professor Maurer, and lastly to Sister Gilda. "You have been a second mother to me, to Matt Busby, Jack Blanchflower, Johnny Berry and all the rest of us," he said, "We can never forget your kindness." Sister Gilda smiled and replied "Goodbye, *aufwiedersehen*, pleasant journey. Come back and see us. God bless you."

With that, he turned and walked to the lift with his wife. As the doors of the lift closed, she was still standing there, smiling and waving, a figure of great strength and compassion, dressed in her black habit and her brilliant white cap.

8

THE AFTERMATH

With the terrible news of the Munich Air Crash came an unprecedented global outpouring of grief. At that time, the world had never before suffered such a terrible sporting disaster and, arguably, it still hasn't. People around the world stood side by side with the people of Manchester and the rest of the country in mourning the loss of so many lives. Words of sympathy and support flooded into the club from royalty, politicians, statesmen, companies, societies and citizens alike. The Queen sent her condolences, as did President Tito of Yugoslavia, the King of Sweden and the Pope. Messages of sympathy came in from the German Chancellor and the French and Italian Ambassadors. Condolences came from some highly unusual sources: the Rector of the University of Bordeaux, the Lirica Italian Opera company, the Soroptimists International Association, the Society of West End Theatre Managers, the Bishop of Chester and Lord Derby.

English football clubs offered to do what they could. Liverpool and Nottingham Forest presented Murphy with a list of players he could sign immediately. Sporting organisations from around the world sent messages of sympathy and offers of support, too. There was international backing for a suggestion made by the president of Red Star Belgrade that Manchester United should be named Honorary Champions of the European Cup for 1958. Some even said the Cup should be renamed the Manchester United Cup. Such was the level of his respect for the club that the great Hungarian Ferenc Puskás, so often England's scourge, offered his services to it with immediate effect, as did his compatriots Zoltan Czibor and Sándor Kocsis, both of whom played alongside Puskás in the Hungarian side that beat England 6-3 at Wembley nearly five years earlier. The day after the disaster, the first of United's overseas supporters clubs was launched in Malta as a mark of respect. Such was the interest in the club from all over the world that many other supporters clubs were started soon after Munich. Today, with an estimated global fan base of approximately 40 million, Manchester United is the richest and best-supported club in the world. It is estimated that 98% of all United's supporters live outside the UK. The Munich Air Crash was the event that single-handedly defined the club and turned it into the world-wide phenomenon that it is today.

In 1958, however, the Munich Air Disaster had left Manchester United Football Club in tatters. Half the first team had been killed and most of those who had survived were not able to play, the Manager was lying gravely ill in hospital, two coaches and the Club Secretary were also dead. All that was left of the club was the Board, the reserves, and Jimmy Murphy. "Jimmy Murphy, in every context carried the club. He kept the whole thing together," says Gregg. From his bed in Munich, Matt Busby had told Murphy to "keep the flag flying, Jimmy, until I get back", and with typical grit and determination, that was exactly what Murphy did.

The first thing he knew he had to do was get Harry Gregg and Bill Foulkes home. They had done the rounds with him in the hospital, trying to cheer the other lads up, but they were clearly beginning to suffer under the strain and needed to get back to their wives and homes. Representatives from BEA offered to fly them back to England at BEA's expense, but their offer was met with incredulity by both players. The last thing they wanted to do was fly. Foulkes said he would never travel again in "a stinking plane". Instead, a passage was booked by train via the Hook of Holland and Harwich.

"We had to make our way back overland with Jimmy," says Harry Gregg. "I remember sitting on the train with a Chinaman in the same compartment as us, you know, sitting on the train in Germany. And Jimmy gibbering away and turned to the old fellow, 'Alright, me old China, can you play?' For the sake of Bill Foulkes and myself, Jimmy taking the mickey for our benefit. It's an act. 'Can you play me old China, what position do you play, we're short of players?' I remember poor old Bill waking up on the ferry coming back from the Hook of Holland screaming and us in the cabin, and me thinking Jesus Christ, what's going on, Bill was screaming in the cabin, having a nightmare. Bill and I saw bad times together, I saw Bill in a bad way and we both lost a terrible lot of weight after the accident. Bill and I returned and played within thirteen days. He [Murphy] was left with two players – Bill Foulkes and myself. And maybe as it was we shouldn't have played, but we did. And I told you about when I climbed the steps, the workers' steps [at the Stachus Hotel], you know those stairs for the staff, and I turned a corner to the top flight and I heard a sobbing and a crying and I looked round the corner and it was Jimmy Murphy sitting crying his eyes out and I turned my back and started down again. The world never seen that face of Jimmy Murphy."

On the train back, Murphy had told them not to think about playing at all, to put it out of their minds for now,

though they all knew that the club was so desperately short
of first team players that Gregg and Foulkes would have to
play sooner or later. Nevertheless, Murphy was worried about
the two of them, particularly Bill Foulkes, who'd reacted to
events after the crash very badly.

The morning after the crash, Gregg and Foulkes were
taken to the airport, where a German official asked them to
give an account of the crash. After that, they were taken to
the scene of the crash to pick up their belongings. Looking
through the wreckage, Harry Gregg found Mark Jones' trilby,
which he picked up and kept. Bill Foulkes went to his seat.
His bag was missing, but in the overhead rack, he found his
briefcase, which was full of magazines, and his overcoat, both
undamaged. In the pocket of his overcoat was the bottle of
gin he'd been given by the Embassy staff in Belgrade. It was
still intact. Foulkes looked around and found a cap with Eddie
Colman's name in it. It had been given to Colman by the
manager of the Continental Club, one of the players' favourite
haunts in Manchester. Foulkes also found Colman's red and
white scarf. Finding these objects upset Foulkes terribly and
he stopped looking for anything else. As he stepped out of the
wreckage, a press photographer took a famous shot of Foulkes
looking gaunt and very uncomfortable.

Gregg and Foulkes were then taken back to the main
airport terminal to identify the luggage that had been salvaged.
Foulkes identified Walter Crickmer's briefcase, which was filled
with cash and traveller's cheques. Also inside was Crickmer's
silver hip flask. Again, finding such personal objects had was
very upsetting for Foulkes. As for Gregg, there was no sign
of his bags and he was left only with the clothes he stood up
in. These, however, were in such a state that, after leaving the
airport, he was taken to a clothes shop back in the city and
bought an entire set of new clothes, including a pair of fur-
lined boots and a beautiful Crombie overcoat.

When their train pulled in at London's Liverpool Street Station, there was a barrage of pressmen and photographers awaiting them. Gregg had never before seen such a large group of pressmen. In the glare of the arc lights, Gregg and Foulkes struggled through the crowds to their wives, who were waiting for them on the platform. United had hired a Rolls Royce, waiting for them outside the station, to take them and their wives back to Manchester. The police helped them leave the station and they slipped into the car. Neither player wanted to travel by train as even that had been a nerve-jangling experience. Every time the train braked, Foulkes broke out in a sweat and was sent into a panic. But the trip in the Rolls did nothing to alleviate his panic attacks and bad nerves. They arrived in Manchester to a hero's welcome, but all they wanted to do was get away from all the attention and be alone.

On the Monday morning after the crash, 21 coffins were taken from the Rechts der Isar Hospital to the airport, where they were loaded onto a BEA Viscount aircraft. A memorial service was conducted on the airfield, with the German Police forming a guard of honour and representatives from several West German football clubs laying wreaths on the coffins. In the afternoon, the plane took off.

Stopping over in London, four coffins were unloaded, including those of Liam Whelan and David Pegg. Whelan's body was flown back to Dublin, where a cortège was waiting to transport the coffin to the city's most famous cemetery, Glasnevin, where Michael Collins and Éamon de Valera were buried. Crowds of people paying their last respects lined the way, from the airport, through the suburb of Santry to the cemetery. The cortège passed his old school, St Peter's, where all the schoolchildren were waiting, and there were so many people congregated at the church that the cortège had difficulty getting through the gates. The actual funeral took place a week after the crash and so many people attended that it was as if another President of Ireland had died.

The Viscount continued on to Manchester, landing at half past nine in the evening. One by one, the 17 remaining coffins were unloaded and put into waiting hearses, watched by family members and friends who had gathered at the airport. Among those there that evening was Harry Gregg. He had been advised by doctors not to attend any of the funerals as the shock might prove too much for his delicate state of mind. But Gregg wanted to see his team mates arrive home and so, against doctor's orders, he had come out to Ringway. Also there that night was Eddie Colman's girlfriend, Marjorie. For her, it was the sight of the coffin that finally made her understand that Colman was dead. The hearses drove off in various directions, but those carrying the bodies of Geoff Bent, Roger Byrne, Eddie Colman, Mark Jones and Tommy Taylor were taken to Old Trafford. Despite the late hour and bad weather, many hundreds of fans stood by the side of the road and paid their last respects to the players. Some even knelt in prayer as the vehicles passed by. As the cortège went through the city, the crowds on the roadsides got larger. Cars stopped in the streets to let the funeral procession by, the inhabitants of every house stood silently outside as a mark of respect. As the hearses approached Old Trafford, the crowd was in tens of thousands. Every patch of spare ground was taken up with people wishing to pay their respects. Along the ten miles from Manchester airport to Old Trafford, an estimated 100,000 people had lined the route.

Once it had got inside the ground, the cortège stopped and the coffins were taken into the gymnasium, which had been turned into a chapel of rest. This is the same gymnasium that Albert Scanlon used to clean out as a junior player, where Roger Byrne had used weights to train with, where Mark Jones used to box and where the players had spent hours playing 'head tennis'. Two policemen were put inside the room to watch over the coffins and the door was locked for the night. Still the crowds congregated at the gates of Old Trafford, placing wreaths on the ground and praying, and it wasn't until the early hours that the last of them returned home. Inside the gymnasium, each coffin had been placed on a table draped in black cloth and in the dusty, windowless room, the smell of varnish was overpowering. One of the policemen, Constable Tom Potter, said years later, "Whenever I smell new varnish I think of those coffins in that gymnasium, and seeing them there with tears in my eyes, and morning couldn't come quick enough so I could go home and try to forget it. But I never have."

When dawn broke, crowds began once again to gather outside the ground. The door to the gymnasium was unlocked and the laundry ladies, Omo and Daz, came inside to polish the coffins. Later on in the morning, club officials gathered inside waiting for relatives as they came to claim the bodies. The first to arrive were Dick and Lizzie Colman. That week was a week of funerals: Henry Rose on Tuesday; Roger Byrne and Frank Swift on Wednesday; Geoff Bent, Tom Curry, Tommy Taylor and Bert Whalley on Thursday; and Eddie Colman, Walter Crickmer and Tom Jackson on Friday. Irene Ramsden and her sister went to a different one each day to pay their respects to the boys they had seen growing up to become beautiful young men. The funeral for Henry Rose was by far the biggest affair. Taxi drivers across the city offered free fares for anyone wishing to attend his funeral at Manchester's Southern Cemetery. So many people went that there was a six-mile queue lining the way for the cortège.

For Murphy, these funerals were terrible, but for the sake of his other players and for the sake of the club, he was determined to concentrate on the job in hand. United had a backlog of league, cup and European fixtures to get through. The Football Association had immediately cancelled

United's league game against Wolves, due to have been played on Saturday 8th February, and allowed United to postpone their fifth round Cup tie against Sheffield Wednesday until 19th February. Murphy therefore had just a week to put together a team.

Like Busby before him, the first thing Murphy did as Manager was to appoint his Head Coach. He knew very well that he would not be able to perform the Herculean task of managing and coaching all by himself, so he got in touch with Jack Crompton, goalkeeper in the famous '48 Cup winning side. At the time, Crompton was Assistant Manager at Luton Town, where he was doing such a good job that Murphy was doubtful he would leave, but when Murphy asked him for his help, Crompton didn't hesitate. He came to Old Trafford immediately and, in fact, was still a trainer at the club when United won the European Cup in 1968.

Crompton's first task was to oversee the unpacking of the large trunk that had arrived from Belgrade and which contained all the playing kit from the game against Red Star. He asked Omo and Daz to clean the shirts, shorts and socks and gave the job of cleaning all the boots to a junior player working on the ground staff called Nobby Stiles. When Stiles had finished, he asked Crompton if he could keep Tommy Taylor's boots as a memento. Crompton said that he could.

With an assistant he could trust in place, Murphy could now afford to turn his attention to the small matter of players. The problem was plain: he simply didn't have enough players to make up a First XI. Playing in goal and at right-back respectively, Harry Gregg and Bill Foulkes were a good start and a solid base on which to build. Out of his reserve players, Ian Greaves, Freddie Goodwin, Ronnie Cope, Colin Webster and Alex Dawson had all played occasionally in the first team and could be called upon to do so again. He decided to give another reserve, Shay Brennan, his first outing in the first team. Usually a left-half, Brennan would play on the left-wing for the game against Wednesday. Desperate as he was, Murphy then considered the juniors. Were any of them at all ready for a first-team game? In all honesty, he knew that none of them were, except one, a young inside-left named Mark Pearson. After much deliberation, he decided to take a chance on Pearson and called him up.

Murphy was still short on numbers, however. He had to look elsewhere. He considered Ferenc Puskás' offer to play for United. It would obviously be a huge draw for United to have in their team a player of such outstanding quality, but there were many drawbacks. Firstly, the FA had placed a ban on foreigners playing in the English leagues and so United would have to find a way of fast-tracking a British citizenship through for Puskás, a process that may raise a few eyebrows and meet a great deal of resistance. On top of that, there was the issue of money. Puskás was earning £800 a week at Real Madrid, whereas the maximum wage for any player at United was £20 a week, a sum that fell to £17 a week during the summer. United would have to find a way of supplementing Puskás' salary, which may well cause some animosity between Puskás and the other players. Although flattered and very tempted by Puskás' offer, Murphy decided not to act on it. Besides being impractical, buying a star player from outside and bringing them into a home-grown team went against everything Busby had set out and managed to achieve at the club. Murphy would have to confine his search to English players.

Within this first week, Murphy hurriedly signed two players to make up numbers. The first was Ernie Taylor, a 33-year old wing-half from Blackpool. Taylor had played for Blackpool in the famous 'Matthews Final' of 1953 and was considered by many to have been the real man of the match that day. Taylor had recently been offered a contract by Sunderland, but Paddy McGrath, Matt Busby's old friend, had persuaded Taylor to meet Murphy over a pint, a meeting during which Murphy convinced Taylor of his need at Old Trafford. Taylor agreed to sign that night and United paid £8,000 for him.

For a fee of £22,000, Murphy also signed Stan Crowther from Aston Villa, a player who had impressed for Villa in the Cup Final the year before. Crowther was not sure of the move, but agreed to travel to Manchester to watch the game against Sheffield Wednesday. Murphy personally met him at the Midland Hotel four hours before the evening kick-off and tried to persuade him to sign. Murphy's passion and enthusiasm succeeded and Crowther agreed to sign on the spot. Crowther had played for Villa in the third round of the FA Cup, and was therefore cup tied for the game that night against Wednesday, but Murphy got in touch with the FA, who waived their usual rules and allowed Crowther to play. The trouble was, Crowther hadn't expected to be playing that night and his boots were in Birmingham, so someone was immediately dispatched to fetch them and managed to get them to Crowther in time for the start of the game. Crowther made his debut for United that night, burdened with the awful responsibility of replacing Duncan Edwards at left-half.

A crowd of 59,848 piled into Old Trafford that Wednesday night, with several thousands more standing silently outside the ground. The team line-up for the game had been printed in the programme before the Munich Air Crash and so the programme had to be completely replaced. Because Murphy had been putting together a team for the match right up to the last minute, he had been unable to give the team sheet to the programme makers earlier that day and so the new programme had not been finished in time. Where the names of United's players for that evening's game should have been listed, the programme instead showed blank spaces, which

said it all. Instead, the players' names were announced over
the tannoy system. The programme did, however, contain a
message from the United Chairman, Harold Hardman:

> On 6 February 1958, an aircraft returning from Belgrade
> crashed at Munich airport. Of the 21 passengers who
> died, 12 were players of officials of the Manchester
> United Football Club. Many other lie injured. It is
> the sad duty of us who serve Manchester United to
> offer our heartfelt sympathy and condolences. Here is
> a tragedy which will sadden us for years to come. But
> in this we are not alone. An unprecedented blow to
> British football has touched the hearts of millions and
> we express our deep gratitude to many who have sent
> messages of sympathy and floral tributes. Wherever
> football is played United is mourned, but we rejoice
> that many of our party have been spared and wish them
> a speedy and complete recovery. Words are inadequate
> to describe our thanks and appreciation of the truly
> magnificent work of the surgeons and nurses of the
> Rechts der Isar Hospital in Munich. But for their superb
> skill and deep compassion our casualties would have
> been greater. To Professor Georg Maurer we offer our
> eternal gratitude. Although we mourn our dead and
> grieve for our wounded we believe that our great days
> are not done for us. The sympathy and encouragement
> of the football world, and particularly our supporters,
> will justify and inspire us. The road back may be long
> and hard but with the memory of those who died at
> Munich, of their stirring achievements and wonderful
> sportsmanship ever with us... MANCHESTER
> UNITED WILL RISE AGAIN.

★ ★ ★

Bill Foulkes was Captain that night and led the team out. Behind him was Harry Gregg. At the sight of these two players walking out onto the pitch, the crowd erupted. Some cheered or shouted out the names of those who had died, others started to cry while a few shrieked hysterically. It was an eerie atmosphere. For the crowd, it was deeply heartening, but also unbearable, to see these two who had survived knowing so many others had lost their lives.

There was a minute's silence before kick-off, and then the rest of the game was a constant chorus of overwrought cheers and cries. The crowd were completely behind United, determined to see their team win on this occasion more than any other. United's progress through the FA Cup was now more of a crusade than anything. It was a measure and a mark of respect to those who had died that United did well. Wednesday were simply overwhelmed by the occasion that night and lost 3-0, with the youngster Shay Brennan scoring twice, one of which was direct from a corner kick. The supporters had shown the club the mass affirmation they needed to win the match and carry on. It was an unforgettably intense occasion.

Amongst the crowd for the Sheffield Wednesday match was Bobby Charlton. Since returning to England a fortnight before, he hadn't felt up to doing much. He whiled away the hours at his family home in Ashington mulling and fretting, going over the same old questions in his mind. Why had all his friends died and not him? Why me? He felt tense, yet drained, and was continually on the verge of tears. He didn't want to meet anyone, or speak to them. The press pestered him for an interview. The family doctor gave him a check-up and pronounced him physically fit. The doctor had a friendly word with Charlton, telling him that life must go on and that he was going to have to start living again sooner or later, but Charlton wanted nothing more to do with football.

After a few more days of this, Charlton decided he would go back to Old Trafford and watch the Wednesday game to see how he felt. He caught the afternoon train down to Manchester and went to a hotel for a meal. Sitting there anonymously, he eavesdropped on the conversations going on around him. Everyone was talking about that evening's game, willing United to win, wanting to see them progress to the next round. People spoke of nothing else. Walking to the ground was strange, but Charlton felt all right. Just before the game, he went into the dressing room to see the others. This was the moment he had been dreading, but Foulkes and Gregg were pleased to see him. Murphy persuaded Charlton to sit next to him during the game, hoping that watching the team get a good result on the night would help Charlton pick up the threads of his football career. He guessed right – it was after that game that Charlton knew he could play again. Charlton said: "But that game against Sheffield Wednesday was more important for what it did for the people of Manchester than for what it did for me."

Two days after the Sheffield Wednesday game, however, news of Duncan Edwards' death spread through the city like a plague, killing the brief euphoria of United's win. Murphy took team to the Norbreck Hydro Hotel in Blackpool where, except for weekends at home with their families, the players stayed for the rest of the season. Manchester was simply too much. The city was still grieving and everyone they saw in the city's streets, pubs, clubs, cinemas and shops still had the look of deep shock on their faces, made worse with the news that Edwards had died. Many still had not begun to come to terms with such a huge loss of life. Old Trafford itself was full of ghosts. Every time the players went into the dressing rooms or on the training pitches, they remembered Bert Whalley and Tom Curry. Every time they went up to the offices, they recalled Walter Crickmer. Most of all, they remembered the seven players, now eight, with whom they would never play again. "We had to get away from Manchester," Bill Foulkes said. "Everyone meant well, of course, but the last thing we needed was their sympathy."

United momentarily had to put the news of Edwards' death out of their minds in order to concentrate on their league game against Nottingham Forest the following day, Saturday 22nd February. Preceding the match at Old Trafford was a memorial service attended by three representatives from Red Star Belgrade, who brought with them gifts to replace the ones destroyed in the crash. Originally intended as a service conducted in memory of those who had died at Munich, this now cruelly included Duncan Edwards, which made the service even more poignant. In the crowd that day was Edwards' fiancée, Molly Leach. The service proved too emotional for her, however, and she had to be taken away before its end. It was decided that the teams should remain in their dressing rooms until the service was over. When it was, the players were greeted by a crowd of 66,123 as they emerged onto the pitch. Unfortunately, the game failed to live up to expectations and finished 1-1.

For these first few games after the crash, however, public interest was not in how well United did in the league – everyone knew it was too late for United to finish high, but the public absolutely willed United to reach the Final and win the Cup. United's next FA Cup match was on Saturday 1st March, a sixth round tie away to West Bromwich Albion. The day before the game, Murphy took his team down to a hotel in Droitwich, near Worcester. In the afternoon, the players went into the hotel lounge, where there was a piano. Murphy's piano playing was legendary and one of the youngsters shouted "Give us a tune, Jimmy", at which point Murphy sat down and entertained the team for the rest of the afternoon by playing Chopin and Liszt.

Although he wasn't match fit, this was the game that marked Bobby Charlton's return to football, less than a month after the crash. At the time, West Brom were one of the best teams in the country, but Murphy knew that, once Charlton came back into the side, United were in with a chance. He was right – Charlton's presence that day gave a huge boost to the team performance and United were ahead most of the game. Four minutes from time, with United leading 2-1, West Brom narrowly avoided defeat by equalising and the game ended 2-2. United's makeshift team had done fantastically well to earn themselves a rematch at Old Trafford in four days' time.

Charlton was now the key player around which Murphy built his side. The replay against West Brom was a finely-balanced match, with the scoreline staying locked at 0-0 for most of the 90 minutes. It looked as though the match was heading for extra time when Ernie Taylor found Bobby Charlton out on the right-hand side. Charlton ran into the box, taking on and beating four defenders before placing the ball across the face of the goal for Colin Webster to score. The whistle blew and United had done it – unbelievably, they were through to the semi-finals of the FA Cup. The dream was still alive. Murphy later said it was one of the proudest moments in his life.

The following morning, two more first-team players arrived back in England from Munich – Kenny Morgans and Dennis Viollet. They too had opted to come back by train via the Hook of Holland into Liverpool Street. When the train pulled in, the scenes were reminiscent of Gregg and Foulkes' return. Ken Morgans' wife, Stephanie, was there to meet them. She says: "It was a right performance at Liverpool Street... there was hundreds of people there and loads of the press and the police, and then some of the police and the reporters got into a fight and somebody's camera got smashed and all the rest of it. Oh, it was a real upheaval. I had a taxi and they let me take it down to the station, you know, ready to sort of meet him. So the train was in and all this rumpus was kicking off outside of the station there and then the police had to make like a gangway to bring Ken and Dennis through."

Back in Manchester, Viollet was finding it difficult to settle into his old life. "The feeling in the town was unbelievable," he said, yet he felt distant from it all, very empty and unhappy. He had grown up with Roger Byrne, Eddie Colman, Dave Pegg and Duncan Edwards, but they were no longer around. "The camaraderie had gone, never to return," he said, "and that was the thing I missed more than anything else. It was more than just team spirit. We would have run through a brick wall for United." To move on from these feelings of lack and loss, Viollet wanted to get back into the first team as soon as he could and so started training straight away, despite the doctors' warning that just a single blow to his head could prove fatal.

Meanwhile, Manchester United had extended an invitation to Professor Maurer and his team to visit Old Trafford so that the club could show them their appreciation for everything they had done and were still doing. Accompanied by his wife and every single member of staff who had treated the players at the Rechts der Isar Hospital, Maurer entered the stadium on Saturday 8th March to watch a league match against West Bromwich Albion. With him, Maurer had brought a tape-recorded message made by Busby for the crowd. Just before the game, the Chairman, Harold Hardman, introduced Maurer to the crowd and then Busby's message was played over Old Trafford's tannoy system. Busby said:

> Ladies and Gentlemen, I am speaking from my bed in
> the Isar Hospital, Munich, where I have been since the
> tragic accident of just over a month ago.

You will be glad, I am sure, that the remaining players here, and myself, are now considered out of danger, and this can be attributed to the wonderful treatment and attention given to us by Professor Maurer and his wonderful staff, who are with you today as guests of the club.

I am obliged to the Empire News for giving me this opportunity to speak to you, for it is only in these last two or three days that I have been able to be told anything about football, and I am delighted to hear of the success and united effort made by all at Old Trafford. Again it is wonderful to hear that the club have reached the semi-final of the FA Cup, and I extend my best wishes to everyone.

Finally, may I just say God bless you all.

It was pure Busby – magnificent words that perfectly fitted the occasion, and the crowd that night wept and cheered at the sentiment his message contained. When the message had finished, the Lord Mayor of Manchester led Maurer and his party out onto the pitch, where they received a standing ovation.

The next FA Cup tie for United was against Fulham at Villa Park, a game played on Saturday 22nd March. The day that United played Fulham, Morgans played a reserve match against Liverpool. Charlton, however, was in the first team and, after just twelve minutes, scored a wonderful goal with a volley from the edge of the penalty area. Fulham equalised, and then went 2-1 ahead, but while one of their players went off for treatment, Charlton scored again, this time off a rebounded shot by Mark Pearson. The game ended 2-2. The last thing they needed was a replay, but at least United were still in it, hanging on by the skin of their teeth. Four days later, United met Fulham again, a game that received so much national interest that it was broadcast live on television.

The match, this time at Highbury, was not particularly well-attended, but was an absolute thriller. Twice United went ahead and twice Fulham pulled them back. After thirteen minutes, Dawson headed the ball in to make it 1-0. Fulham equalised, but Dawson slipped another past the Fulham keeper soon afterwards. Three minutes later, Fulham equalised again, but the 20-year-old Brennan put United 3-2 up three minutes later. Dawson scored his hat-trick nineteen minutes into the second half to put United into a seemingly unassailable 4-2 lead. But the game wasn't over when Fulham scored again, making it 4-3. With fifteen minutes to go, however, Charlton scored another one of his trademark volleys from just outside the area to finish the game 5-3. Despite all the adversity and against all the odds, United were through to their second FA Cup Final in two years. It was another unbelievable result and one that confirmed the charmed progress United were making in the FA Cup.

United's victory was greeted around the country with unalloyed joy. In Munich, too, United's path to the final was received with pure glee. Busby sent a message from the hospital to the club, saying "Tell Jimmy I am delighted. Tell him to keep it up." The result reinvigorated Busby and he was now determined to make it back to England in time for the final, which, with typical aplomb, he did. On 19th April 1958, 71 days after the crash, he set foot back in England. The first week he spent convalescing at home with his family, after which he called a meeting at Old Trafford in order to wish the players well for the final. Privately, though, Busby was terrified of returning to Old Trafford. On the appointed day, the players and staff gathered in the physio room, underneath the stands. They all watched as Busby entered the room on crutches. Many noticed how the crash had aged him. Omo

and Daz both gave him a kiss on the cheek. With Jimmy
Murphy and Jack Crompton flanking him, Busby began to
address the players but stopped almost immediately. He tried
to speak again, but broke down sobbing instead. He was led
away by Murphy and Crompton. It was a difficult moment
for Busby, but at least he had exorcised his fear of returning
to the ground. It would be better next time.

The Cup Final was played at Wembley on 3rd May. United's
opponents in the final were Bolton Wanderers, who have
always been one of United's 'bogey' teams, but the country
was behind United that Saturday. The club's extraordinary
run in the cup contained within it all the ingredients for
a dream end to the nightmare – it seemed destined to be
United's day. Kenny Morgans pronounced himself fit enough
to play the game, but Murphy decided otherwise and didn't
call him up. "I was very disappointed," Morgans says, "very
disappointed." Taking his place was Dennis Viollet, who had
already played his first match since the crash – the Cup Final
was his second. Although he wasn't yet match-fit, Viollet's
top-level experience and natural ability would surely count
for a lot on the day and his inclusion was a further tonic for
the team.

Just before kick-off, the teams remained in their dressing
rooms while the crowd sang a particularly heartfelt "Abide
With Me". Bolton and United, led out by Murphy, then
emerged onto the pitch to a rapturous welcome. United were
in their familiar red shirts but, for this match only, the United
shirts had been specially embroidered with a phoenix rising
from the ashes. The Duke of Edinburgh shook hands with the
players and then the whistle blew to start the game.

Within just three minutes, however, Nat Lofthouse put
the ball past Harry Gregg and into the back of United's
net. It was the worst possible start for United, but everyone
watching in the ground and around the country on television

hoped that it would inspire them to get back into the game. Unfortunately, it didn't, and the teams went off the pitch at half time with the score still 1-0. A few minutes after the restart, Bolton came at United again. Harry Gregg parried a shot and was gathering the ball from the air when Lofthouse charged him in the back and the ball popped out of Gregg's arms and into the back of his own goal. The challenge was clearly a foul – even Lofthouse expected the referee to give a free kick – but the referee blew for a goal instead. It was the death knell for United's FA Cup hopes and they never recovered. For the second successive year, a controversial challenge on United's keeper had settled the FA Cup Final. Controversy aside, however, the truth of the matter was that, on the day, United were soundly beaten by Bolton Wanderers. Despite the build-up and the good wishes of the country, the final was a dispiriting experience for Harry Gregg:

"Bill Foulkes and I played thirteen days after the crash. Now to play in the English cup, you're really emotional, you're built up, you're keyed up. I played against Sheffield Wednesday and against all the odds we beat 'em, we drew West Brom, we had two games, one there we drew and we beat them at home. Now at any other time in your life – and we went on to qualify, there was nobody in the team apart from Bill and eventually Bobby and myself and I swear to you, to get to Wembley is the biggest thing in most people's lives. Every game, after what happened to do with the accident, was an anticlimax. Any other time in your life you'd have been walking about, you played the game, you put everything into it, you put more into it than what you had, but we're back to asking me what did it feel like. I must say that period, from then, achieving what the team achieved with most of the team dead and most of the reserves dead, even after those achievements which were unbelievable, it was an anticlimax. Wembley meant nothing to me, where before I'd been at Wembley, it would have been the greatest. We met the Duke of Edinburgh, he was on the pitch and when you're really keyed up it's just... It was an anticlimax because of what had happened at that time."

Back in Manchester, United boarded an open-top bus at Manchester's Victoria Station and did a tour of the city to the Town Hall. Along the way, thousands upon thousands of well-wishers waved and cheered at them. Albert Square was full with an estimated 100,000 people, all of whom had turned out to show the players and the club solidarity in the face of defeat. It was almost 50 years since United had won their first FA Cup and were taken along the same route by horse-drawn carriage, and ten years since the famous team of '48 had triumphed for a second time. For what was left of the Busby Babes, though, defeat in United's third final was bitter. Bill Foulkes felt particularly disappointed for all the people standing in front of him. He had wanted more than anything to bring the Cup home for them. As captain, he had to stand up and say a few words to the crowd. He went through the motions, but at the same time, he thought to himself "I can't stand any more of this." Later on in the Town Hall, with the crowds outside still shouting for the players, Foulkes sat down with Busby and Murphy and started sobbing. It was all catching up with him.

Once again, however, United had to find the inner strength from somewhere to pull themselves together for one last commitment – a European Cup semi-final against AC Milan to be played at Old Trafford the following Wednesday. Bobby Charlton had been called up to play for England in a friendly against Portugal the same night and, when United put their case forward for Charlton to play in the semi-final, the Football Association refused. Indeed, the FA told United that Charlton would not be available for the return leg, either, because of international duty. Despite this massive setback, United still managed a 2-1 win on the night, with Viollet scoring his first goal since returning. A week later, however, events since the Munich Air Crash finally caught up with United and they were thrashed 4-0 at the San Siro. They had come to the end of the road.

As a gesture of sympathy and support for the club, UEFA invited Manchester United to enter the European Cup the following year, regardless of their league position at the end of the season. The decision wasn't United's to make, however, it was the FA's. Realising that they had perhaps been too severe with United over Charlton's participation in the European Cup semi-final, the FA allowed United to accept UEFA's invitation. Football's other governing body, the Football League, had other ideas, though, and protested the decision, saying that, as Champions, Wolves were the only team eligible for entry into the European Cup. Busby appealed the decision to the FA, who backed Busby, but the Football League, a body made up of club Chairmen, stood firm – rules were rules, after all. The two controlling authorities of English football remained at loggerheads and a huge row broke out, but without the approval and support of the Football League, the FA had no alternative but to give up its position – United would not be allowed to enter the European Cup.

The decision was a bitter blow for the club and Busby, in particular, took it very personally. Following so quickly after the letdown of losing the Cup Final, it seemed that nothing was going United's way. In reality, however, so depleted were United that they were in no position to make a serious claim on any of the major competitions. United's bubble had finally burst and the realisation that United would have to start again completely from scratch began to sink in. When Matt Busby left hospital, he was asked how long it would take him to rebuild his team. "Five years," he said. In 1958, they had finished ninth in the league, the following year they were runners-up to Wolves, in 1960 they dropped back down to tenth place, their eventual finishing place the year after that, too. In 1962, United finished fifteenth and were in danger of being relegated. The following year, they struggled all season to stay up. In all of this time, they did nothing at all in the FA Cup. There were whisperings that Busby could not manage to build another successful team, but neither Busby nor Murphy panicked – they had been here before. Busby was building a team around his key player, Bobby Charlton, and knew that it took time for a new team to gel.

That year, 1963, was a strange year – although struggling again for survival in the league, United were doing well in the Cup, beating Huddersfield Town, Aston Villa and Chelsea on their way to the sixth round. Frank Taylor was once again covering football matches for his paper and, reporting on United's sixth-round cup tie against Coventry, Taylor sent a postcard of Coventry Cathedral to Frank Kessel back in Munich predicting that United would win it that year. He had no evidence for his prediction – it was just a gut feeling. Kessel said that if that was the case, could he get a ticket for the final for him? Taylor said he would.

Sure enough, United beat Coventry in the sixth round and went on to beat Southampton in the semi-finals – they had made it to the Final, where they would meet Leicester City. Busby was more than happy to give Kessel a ticket and also invited him to United's Cup Final dinner at the Savoy in the evening. Kessel, one of Europe's top neurological surgeons and self-styled Chairman of the Munich branch of the Manchester United Supporters' Club, was beside himself with excitement as he sat next to Taylor at Wembley.

Taylor and Busby were both right on the mark with their prediction. In 1963, exactly five years after the crash, United won the FA Cup, beating Leicester City 3-1. It was the game in which Denis Law announced his presence on the world stage of football. Kessel was overjoyed, saying "I am so happy to be here to see the final act after the tragedy in Munich."

A few months after that, a youngster from Belfast, George Best, made his first- team debut. Slowly, United were beginning to cohere into another great team – Busby's third – and its pinnacle was winning the European Cup in 1968. In the Final, held at Wembley, United completed the *bona fide* last act of the Munich Air Crash by beating Benfica 4-1 after extra time, with Bobby Charlton scoring two goals. When the final whistle blew and United had won, Matt Busby, who had coveted the European Cup for twelve years, came onto the pitch with his arms aloft. Charlton walked towards him and they embraced on the field. Both men broke down amidst the jubilant crowd, and the other, exhausted players. Busby and Charlton's thoughts were not with those around them at that moment, however – they were back in Munich, on the snowy expanses of the airport and the brilliant young lives lost there that day.

The Munich Air Disaster drew very close together all those who went through the harrowing events of that day but, afterwards, it was also an event that placed a great distance between each of them and kept them apart in the years following. Growing up together, and sharing all the experiences that life as a footballer had to offer a group of inseparable young men, the crash suddenly destroyed their safe and secure environment. Each man who went through that experience and came out the other side was labelled a "survivor", a tag which all of them grew to mistrust. The sudden loss and the guilt of having lived where others had inexplicably died – these two dreadful feelings were obscured by the magnitude of the tag. They should have been happy to survive, and of course they were, but in reality, they also lived under a huge burden for many years to come, a burden that caused a great deal of unhappiness in the rest of their lives.

Above all, Harry Gregg and Albert Scanlon are both proud and honoured to have played alongside the Busby Babes. As a final testament to the players who died in Munich, perhaps we should let them be better remembered for how they played, not for how they died. The last words are Albert Scanlon's:

"And as you go on in the years – it's not happened for a long time – if they decide at Old Trafford to invite you and they invite like David Pegg's sister and her husband and Eddie's father and mother or Mrs Byrne or Mrs Bent, you always have the feeling they are looking at me, thinking why's he stood there and my lad's dead? As soon as I walked in any room, Mr Colman would look at me, you know. And he was an only child, Eddie, and I was an only child. And I think it broke his mother's heart in the end. And then when I went to work on the docks, Eddie's dad was on the docks but he worked for the railways and he was very, very bitter. But you sit down later and you think, but if it hadn't have happened, he'd have been a proud man that his son would have probably gone on to play for England and this is just a one-off… It's been a long time. I wouldn't know what happened to the sons and the daughters. I believe Eddie, Tommy and David burnt to death in the toilets, they locked themselves in the toilets, and I wouldn't know how they died, all I know that they was dead. And yet Harry actually found Bobby and Roger – there wasn't a mark, only a little cut above his eye had Bobby, and yet Roger had broken his back. You know, when people ask you, 'Oh, were you in the air…?' They still ask today. They say, 'No, you weren't there'. And you say, 'Yeah, I was there'. 'Yeah, but you didn't play.' You say, 'Yeah, I played'. Because I told you before, the thing they show is the fifty-seven side, which won the championship. They were brilliant players, but so were the lads that I played with. Both teams were the same, it was only like Greggy, Kenny, Bobby, Mark and myself that had gone in [for the match against Leicester City on 21st

December 1957]… and it gets harder as years go on, 'cos you
don't forget these people. I can picture 'em now, as they was
then, and that's the only way I really like to remember them.
The little quirks they had and I can remember them all. And
how they looked on that day, I can remember all that. I can
see it, I can see it in front of me, you know, I just sit here
some nights and have a smoke and have a read and I can start
off then. And it's as though somebody shoves a slide in across
your brain, I can just turn it on and I can see 'em play. I get
a lot of it in the pubs – what was he like and what was he
like? And I always say to 'em, if you didn't see, they cannot
be described, but there's nobody today better. You know,
like Roger, Tommy, Dennis, all these people. There's nobody
playing football today better than them."